Investing Kindergarten

Investing
Kindergarten

THE SIMPLE TRUTH THAT'S
WORTH A FORTUNE

James Pavoldi ARM, ALCM

ISBN-13: 9781977910790
ISBN-10: 1977910793

Dedication

This book is my advice to my children and grandchildren. I really do wish I knew this information 50 years ago! If I did, I would most certainly be a multimillionaire today! What I have learned is worth a fortune, and I want my sons James and Nicholas to have it in a nutshell. Here it is boys; read every word, learn it and pass it on to your children. Most importantly, implement what you learn here as quickly as possible. This book should be mandatory reading.

Disclaimer

I believe the information in this book to be accurate, but make no warrantee or guarantee of accuracy. My words in no way offer individualized advice, nor do they recommend any specific portfolio. Ideas are presented but should not be taken as individual investment advice. If you require individual investment, legal, or accounting advice, you should seek out the professionals with expertise in those disciplines. I have made every attempt to be accurate with the data included in this text, but you should be aware that any and all past performances cited do not suggest or guarantee future performance. Rules, laws, and guidelines, can and do change with time. Always check on the most current rules, laws, and guidelines. While this book does cite some specific companies, it is in no way endorsing any particular organization, nor does it recommend or offer for sale any security. No securities should be purchased without first reading and understanding fully the prospectus provided for that security. The author disclaims any liability and responsibility for any losses that anyone may sustain. All investments expose the investor to potential gains and losses. I am not, nor do I present myself as a financial advisor. Investing always involves risk, and therefore should only be done with the utmost of care and caution. This book is a collection of ideas and opinions, not recommendations, and should be taken as such. It is guidance that I have organized to help my family understand investing.

Table of Contents

CHAPTER 1

Congratulations! Simply picking this book up means you are serious about your financial future. By reading it, you will know more about investing finance than 99% of the world's population. This information is worth a fortune. I have kept it very short and simple so that you will be more likely to read it completely. I will explain everything in plain English, just as if we were chatting over a cup of coffee.

I wrote this book for the benefit of my family. When a father or mother knows something important, it is their inclination to tell their children. That is just what parents do. We want our children to have every advantage. In my case, what I have learned about investing in the last 45 years is so valuable, I had to write it down to be sure my sons would have it in a concise form. This book distills 45 years of experience into some simple conclusions that I want my family to fully understand.

I would like to start out with something that should help motivate the reader to accumulate "money machines". Money machines are just that, instruments that produce money.

Let me share a short but very powerful story that should help to put this concept into focus.

A twelve-year-old boy was asked to sit down with his father. His father was an Italian Immigrant who had come to the United States with nothing. The father said that the boy was to listen carefully to what he was about to be told. Here is what the father told his young son:

"What I am about to say is so important, it must never be forgotten. It is the kind of information that that will change your life. Remember these words and pass them on to your children."

With that, the man outstretched his arms palm side up.

"When I came to this country, I had nothing. I had no money, and nothing to sell except my hands, my sweat, and my heartbeats. Put your hands on top of mine and tell me what you feel."

The boy placed his hands on his father's upturned hands. His father's hands were heavily calloused and rough. The boy told his father that his hands felt like the bark of a tree.

"These are the hands that I sold. They have laid up over a million bricks and blocks. All I had to sell was these hands and my understanding of masonry. I had very little formal schooling, but I knew how to mix concrete, and how to read a level and square. I knew how to build a wall straight and true. I knew how to form an arch with stone that could support a building. People were willing to pay me for my hands, and for the little bit of knowledge that I possessed. I did not know much, but what I knew, I knew well, and understood with all my heart, and in every fiber of my being. Now my son ... hear and understand this, for I have learned another thing well, and it is what I will teach you today. What I am about to tell you is worth a fortune. I don't say that with any exaggeration, or arrogance. I'm about to tell you something that very few people your age ever hear, and even fewer understand. I almost feel as if I am telling you a great secret."

At this point, the father poured himself a glass of wine and poured a small amount into a shot glass which he handed to his son. This was a ceremony, and it was designed to be etched into the boy's mind.

"Take a sip of wine. I want to show you something."

The man and the boy took sips of wine, and the father continued his speech.

"Take this and look at it," he said as he handed the boy an impressive looking certificate. It was elegant. The calligraphy and artwork made it look like it should be framed, and hung on a wall. The edges were gilded, and the entire thing had the feel of something extraordinary.

"What you have in your hand is the very first stock certificate that I ever owned. They don't issue them like this anymore. Now everything is done differently. Stocks are just numbers in an account. But I saved this certificate so I could give it to you, and you will have it to show to your children. This is a very important part of your education, and it is your responsibility to pass it on.

The certificate was issued from Coca Cola. It indicated that the holder of the certificate owned five shares of stock.

"What you hold in your hand does not sweat like me. It does not hurt like I do after a day of work. It doesn't get rough and leathery as my hands are after years of lifting bricks to make money. No, it just produces income like a little money machine. If you own enough of these machines, they can make more money than your father's hands. Do you understand this? Shares like these will pay for your college education. They will allow your mother and me to retire and enjoy life without back breaking work. I have always used a part of what these hands made to buy pieces of wonderful American companies. These are like very special machines because they make more of themselves the longer you own them. It is important that you understand this. Time multiplies these things, and they grow in numbers as the years go by. You must begin to buy money machines as early as you can because the longer you own them, the more they make of themselves. This is a form of mathematical magic."

After taking another sip of wine, and instructing his son to do likewise, the father displayed a leather handled mason trowel to his son.

"This trowel has laid up tens of thousands of bricks. It has helped me to make a lot of money, but it can only make money when it is in my hand, and moved by my arm and my strength. I dip it into the mortar, I deposit the mix onto a brick and then use it to sweep away the excess. I tap the brick level with the handle. I do that over and over again until my trowel, my strength, the bricks, and mortar have made something that will last for generations."

He did all of this while making the exact moves with his trowel as if he were laying a row of bricks. This action was done with the smoothness and grace that comes from doing something hundreds of thousands of times. He then continued.

"It is a good and honorable tool. It put food on our table and a roof over our heads, but it could do none of that without my hand, and the strength of my arm. When I wipe it clean, and set it in my work bag, it could stay there for a hundred years, and it will not make a penny. That is not the case with these money machines, he said once again, handing the stock certificate to his son. They produce money day and night, week after week, year after year. They multiply and make more of themselves. Much like a plant that produces seeds to make more of itself, these money machines produce seeds called dividends that buy more and more shares for you as the years progress. Over a very long time, they can be worth millions. To them, time is magic. This magic is called compounding, and it is how a man like me, who started out poor, can eventually become wealthy. Unlike a man, who loses strength as he ages, these money machines gain strength and produce more as time passes. Money machines work for you nonstop. They work when you sleep, when you rise, and when you go about life. They work when you can no longer work yourself. It is your responsibility to accumulate them as early as possible so that this incredible process can begin."

The father swallowed the last of the wine and set the empty glass down hard.

"You see this empty glass? This is what you will have in old age unless you do as I am instructing you. Never spend all that you make. Use some of your earnings to buy money machines. When I worked in the hot sun for ten hours a day, I invested two hours pay into money machines. Someday, those money machines will do all my work for me. I will rest in the shade, but I will keep this trowel to remind me of my humble beginnings. Respect the tools and the skills that you earn a living with.

Never substitute excuses for saving. There will always be a reason to postpone saving. Every one of those reasons lays out a path to poverty. It is a path well-trodden, and one you must never take. Let my words stay in your heart and mind. Do you understand?"

With that, the son drained the last few drops of wine from the shot glass. He set it down hard. Then, tipping it upside down for emphasis, he looked his father squarely in the eyes, and said: "Yes."

It is my hope that by the end of this short book, you too will say *yes*. Yes, you understand the importance of accumulating money machines, and yes, you know how to do it efficiently. I believe low cost index funds are the most efficient way to accumulate money machines. (stocks) Investing does not need to be complicated or expensive. Actually, when it comes to investing, simplicity and efficiency are proving to be the best course.

CHAPTER 2

Accumulating a Retirement Fortune is Much Easier Than You Think

First, stop giving away up to 50% of your investment earnings. (Yes ... millions of people do it!) What? Who would do that? No one in their right mind would give away 30%, 40% or even 50% of their investment earnings, would they? Yes, they will, and they do. In fact, many people who are invested right now are giving away a substantial percentage of their earnings. Most have no idea how much, or even how it is taken from them. (They don't actually "give it away", they pay it out in fees and expenses.) The net result is the same. The money leaves their account, never to return.

Let me explain. I'll use a simple example to keep the math easy. Say $10,000 is invested with a full-service broker, who charges 1.25% for managing the portfolio. That doesn't sound too bad, after all, the broker knows a lot more about this stuff than the average investor. The broker has the account invested in four different mutual funds, each of which charge 0.75% for expenses. Again that sounds cheap since the folks who run those funds can, and often do, make double-digit returns. Here's the problem: 1.25% +0.75% equals 2%. If the gross amount of gain is just 4% over the course of one year, and it cost 2% of the portfolio value in fees, that means $200 of the $400 in gains went to fees. ($10,000 x .02=$200) **That $200 is 50% of the yearly earnings!**

I'll repeat that because it's important; **50% of the earnings** gets paid out in fees. *Let's do the math.* The total portfolio gain is **$10,000 x 4% = $400. If 2% is paid** out in fees, those fees must be deducted from the $400 in gross gain. That leaves you with just $200, or

Some investors have given away 50% of their one year gains!

Expenses are often overlooked because they don't sound like much, but that can be a terribly costly mistake.

Accounts grow much larger When less is taken out of them to pay fees.

50% of your original gain. **The money was invested for an entire year to earn 4%, but in the end, you only realize 50% of that amount after the combined fees from the broker and the fund managers! Half of your earnings go to others!**

Of course, if the gross returns are higher, the percentage of your gains paid out to fees goes lower. For example, if the return is 10%, the math would be: $10,000 x 10% =$1,000. Since the fees are $200, we divide $200 by $1,000 to get 20%. (That's still a huge chunk of the yearly gains being paid out in fees!)

I know what people are thinking: "Hey! Wait a minute. How did we pay 50% of our gain when the broker only charges a measly 1.25%? This is beginning to sound a bit confusing!"

Yes, it is confusing. Yes, the portfolio management fee is only 1.25%. That 1.25% is charged against the entire amount of investments under management. In this case, the amount of assets being managed is $10,000. 1.25% x $10,000 is $125. Since the mutual funds all charge.75%, we must calculate $10,000 x.75%. That equals $75. When those 2 fees are added together, they equal $200. Since the entire portfolio gained 4%, and 4% x $10,000 is $400, we need to deduct the $200 of expenses from the gross gain. The net gain becomes $200, or 50% of the gross gain. (Is this all beginning to make sense now?) How would anyone feel who did a job for $400 and got paid $200 after expenses?

Think about that for a minute. Your investing goal is to compound money as quickly and efficiently as possible. One way to achieve that is to keep investing expenses low. In my personal accounts, **I keep almost 100% of my earnings** because I pay no broker management fees, and I use very low-cost index funds. Believe me, that makes a huge difference.

If the market undergoes a correction, (a drop of 10% or more), and your funds go down by 10%, you lose an additional 2%, since you pay fees regardless of whether the market goes up or down. At this point, your net loss is not 10% but 12%. Regardless of what the market does, that 2% paid out in fees is a big piece of invested money that disappears. Never underestimate how damaging the loss of 2% can be. When markets are relatively flat, and gains are only in the 3% or 4% range, that 2% in fees is devastating. If the stock market has a soft year and only returns 2%, the net gain after expenses will be **zero.**

Bear in mind that fees go on year after year. If the first 2% of a portfolio goes to fees, the portfolio must overcome that before any gains are made. What if, instead of paying 200 basis points, (2%), the account was self-managed and invested in an index fund costing just 7 basis points? That's what I do. Instead of paying 50% of the profits in fees, (on a 4% gain), I get to keep nearly 100% of my earnings. My total cost for $10,000 invested in an index fund charging 7 basis points is just $7. Instead of paying $200 for management and fees, I pay just seven bucks per year! That's less than 2 cents a day on $10,000. All that extra gain gets re-invested and will continue to grow and multiply in my account for decades! Investing like that provides a very powerful edge. Wealth will grow a great deal faster. I will demonstrate how that seemingly insignificant 2% could result in a difference of hundreds of thousands of dollars! By the way, not many things about investing can be stated categorically as a sure thing. Expenses, however, are something that can be shopped for, measured, and controlled. Reducing expenses can drastically improve long-term returns.

Let's say that $10,000 is invested, along with an additional $500 a month for 40 years. With very low expenses, say 0.09%, instead of 2.00%, at the end of 40 years, the account will have accumulated **$1,728,098.53** on an 8% yearly return. (no taxes calculated) That same portfolio with a 2% fee will yield **$696,669.56** less! May I repeat that for emphasis? Just paying that 2% out in expenses will result in almost **seven hundred thousand dollars** less! Somebody got that $696,669.56 … just

not you! Think about that for a minute. Think about it because it could change your life. It could change the way you live when you reach my age. (66 years old.) It will be too late then to get that money back. You will wonder then why someone didn't warn you. Well, you have now been warned! At the risk of being redundant, let me explain what that means in terms of income. At age 66, you start drawing out 4% of the portfolio as a pension. *(4% is a commonly recommended withdrawal rate.)*[1] The low expense portfolio provides an income of $69,123.94 per year. The high expense portfolio provides an income of $41,257.15. Read that again. It is very important to understand how much difference expenses make over long periods of time. In this case, the period was 40 years. Why would anyone want to have a retirement income of $41,257.15 per year, when they could just as easily have $69,123.94? (Said another way, why settle for a retirement income of $793 a week when it is just as easy to have $1,329 a week?) Who would not want to invest in a way to make the higher yearly income, especially when the only difference

---

1 The assumption is that your account will continue to earn some returns, so keeping your withdrawal down to 4% should extend the length of time your funds will last. If you earn more than 4%, your account may actually grow as you draw on it.

is the fees paid during that 40-year period of accumulation?

Believe me, two percentage points over long periods of time make an incredible difference. Here is another example: Let's say a 21-year-old decides to put $300 per month into a 401(k). If that account earns 8% yearly, by age 66, the account should have a total of $1,391,420.22. (Calculations are without taxes or fees.) If the account earned 10%, the total would be $2,588,057.41. Look at the difference just 2% makes! Do you see now why I have absolutely no desire to pay out 2% in fees?

Let me put it another way. Having a portfolio with high fees is like running a race-car with low octane gasoline. Running one with extremely low fees is like racing with nitromethane. Nitromethane fuel carries some oxygen to enhance combustion. A low expense portfolio carries all that extra money never paid out in fees, and that money compounds to make the account grow faster.

A person retiring with $2.5 million is going to have a much more luxurious retirement than a person who has just $1.4 million. Incredibly the only difference between them is the 2% in fees. By the way, this example is a working-class person putting away just $300 per month for 45 years. In all likelihood, wages will go up with time, and so will the monthly savings. It is not impossible; in fact, it's very easy, for an average working-class person to be able to accumulate large sums of money to retire with, providing they start out very early. I must emphasize again here, that *time* is the magic.

Now let me be clear, I have nothing personal against full-service brokers or financial advisors. I know lots of them, and most are wonderful people who work hard and want clients to be successful in their investments. They can and do provide valuable services. A full-service broker may advise a client away from making very bad investments. For example, a client becomes convinced that a stock she has heard about is the opportunity of a lifetime, and wants to buy it for her portfolio. The broker may look at the stock, analyze its numbers, and advise the client to steer clear of that investment. That advice may save the investor from making a serious mistake. The broker might very well save that client far more than the 1.25% they charged for management. If, in such a case, the broker saved the client from a 60% loss, the 1.25% paid for that advice will have been money well spent.

Some of the other services that brokers, and financial advisors provide are as follows:

1: They help evaluate the level of appropriate risk for every age.
2: They can help investors select funds that will fit into their goal and risk criteria.

3: They can advise on financial strategies, and help make certain there will be enough liquidity for withdrawals when needed.

4: They will provide clients with calming, reassuring words when the market gets volatile and investments fluctuate wildly. Many full-service brokers have prevented their clients from making serious and costly mistakes during market downturns. They deserve credit for that.

The services they provide are not free, but if you feel that you need them, and some people do, then employ them at the lowest cost you can negotiate. Be sure to let them know that you are very concerned about fees and expenses. Tell them you need to know exactly how much the fees are on a quarterly, and yearly basis. Make sure they know that you want investments with very low expense ratios.

I know that not everyone is cut out to manage their own investments. Some people just do not have the temperament. They tend to over-react and may do more harm than good for themselves if they try to manage their own money. Some folks just don't want to be bothered by it all; they prefer to have someone else do it for them. Some investors don't understand the business, and don't want to learn about it. These people should use financial professionals. Just remember, most people would not hire a lawn service to mow and trim their property unless they knew how much that service will cost on a yearly basis. It baffles me why people hire financial professionals without ever asking how much *it* will cost on a yearly basis.

My position is that I simply don't need them, and millions of investors may not either, once they understand some very simple concepts. Today, anyone can achieve the same, and sometimes better results on their own using very low-cost funds, *(Index funds, ETF's, or low cost mutual funds)*. By saving on expenses, the difference in wealth accumulation over time is astounding. My point in this discussion is not to disparage the financial services industry, but to point out that there is ***no free lunch***. Money management comes at a cost, and that cost can reduce portfolio growth quite significantly over time.

New investors often need help and guidance as they begin the process of growing a fortune. One option to consider is hiring a fiduciary. What is a fiduciary? I'm so glad you asked! A fiduciary is legally obligated to act in your best interest. It is not enough for a fiduciary to advise clients on an investment that will be *suitable* for them. The fiduciary will charge a flat fee for her advice, but that advice must always be in the best interest of the client. If a total stock market mutual fund with an expense ratio of 1.23% would be suitable, but an index fund can be had to do the same thing for an expense ratio a full percentage point less, the fiduciary will advise the client to buy the index fund. That is clearly in the client's best interest. The fiduciary is not "selling" anything. She is an advocate. She is there to advise, and she is legally bound to maintain the client's best interest. She doesn't work for free, but neither does a plumber. She may have expertise that an investor needs, especially at the beginning of an investment journey. What I am talking about here is a *fee-only advisor*.[2] Those exact words are important. A *fee-only advisor* is not allowed to take commissions or payments from third parties. No one is pushing her to sell a particular mutual fund, bond, or any other vehicle. She only recommends something if your best interest is satisfied. A *fee-only advisor* may advise clients to sell some investment generating 2% annually, in order

2 New investors with tiny accounts may find that advisors are not willing to take them on as clients. Since many advisors get paid based on a percentage of money under management, a tiny account will not pay them enough. You may be able to pay a straight fee for advice though.

to pay off a credit card debt costing 21% annually. She may recommend this action even if it means she will make less money from the account she is managing. (She is paid a percentage of investments under management.) She is being paid to do what is best for the client. *Gee ... you never heard about any of this before!* I wonder why? Who did you think was going to tell you? I have absolutely nothing to gain by any of the information I provide. I am not in the financial business, nor do I represent any company or organization. My only objective in writing this book is so my children and grandchildren will have the critical and often hidden information that it took me too long to find and figure out for myself. I would be derelict of my parental duty if I failed to provide this information to my children, even though they are grown men.

An organization called NAPFA, (National Association of Personal Financial Advisors), can help you find a fee-only advisor near you. They have a website which I strongly recommend: www. napfa.org. This site will provide lots of helpful information about fiduciaries, and how to find and evaluate them. There are financial education videos, webinars, articles, and much more. It is a great place to go to understand the fundamentals of smart investing.

Here is a very important point regarding 401(k) plans provided by the workplace. 401(k) administrators may be selected by the employer, which means you may not have a lot to say about expenses and fund choices. It is still a good idea to question, and be aware of all expenses related to the plan. Having said that, *by all means, maximize your participation in your 401(k).*

Note: *For those not familiar with ETFs, mutual funds, index funds, stocks, bonds, 401(k)'s, and IRAs, you may want to jump ahead to chapters 5 and 6 where I explain these things in simple terms. One of the fundamental rules of investing is to know and understand everything about what you have invested your money in. Just knowing a stock symbol, and generally what a company does, is not enough. Chapter 5, will explain mutual funds, index funds, ETFs, stocks, and bonds. It's not very complicated. I compare mutual funds, index funds, and ETFs, with individual stocks and bonds. I explain about IRAs, 401(k)s and Roth IRAs in chapter 6. Remember, this is investors' kindergarten, so we're going to keep it simple and easy to understand. Remember also that building wealth is like building a house. If you don't know the difference between a truss, a joist, a header, and a rafter, you aren't ready to do any building at all. So, if you want a better understanding of the building blocks of investing, jump right over to chapters 5 and 6, and in just a few minutes I will demystify these investment concepts for you.*

(Whatever you do, don't skip reading any of this book. All of it needs to be understood completely.)

OK. Investing your nest egg without paying high fees and expenses can be done using a discount broker and buying index funds, ETFs, or low expense ratio mutual funds.

(Of course, individual stocks can be bought at low-cost, but that does take a lot more skill and experience.) Here are a few names of discount brokers to consider:

DISCOUNT

Discount brokers have made it possible for anyone to have access to the stock market for the lowest cost possible.

This is a new age and new era for investors.

Fidelity, Charles Schwab, Vanguard, E-Trade, TD Ameritrade, TradeKing, and Interactive Brokers.

I use Fidelity, and I am always amazed at the wonderful tools and research they provide for free. All of these discount brokers do a good job providing support. Once an account is opened, there will be a plethora of ETFs, index funds, and mutual funds from which to choose. Which funds you choose will make all the difference in the world. Deciding on the right funds is where some professional guidance may be a good idea. Lots of things need to be considered, including your age, time frame, and risk profile. Getting on the correct trajectory is very important. Most discount brokers will be able to provide some guidance. You may have to pay for that service, but it is important that all resources are allocated in a way that best meets your needs and objectives. While this is not complicated, it does require experience that an investor may not have when they begin the investment journey. A discount broker may have a CFP (certified financial planner), or a CFA, (chartered financial analyst) on staff that can help get the process started. Just remember, if someone is managing your account, they will charge a fee, and that fee will be a drag on all future gains. If a portfolio of low-cost index funds or ETF's can meet your needs, you really don't need to pay anyone a management fee to babysit that portfolio. An occasional review to ensure that the allocations still meet your goals is a good idea. Discount brokers provide lots of tools at no cost that are very helpful.

It is when people first begin to invest that they often get locked into management arrangements where they tend to remain in for years without any further thought or question. When the account is tiny, the expenses don't amount to much. Once the account starts getting larger, the expenses grow because they are based on a percentage of the account's total value.

ETFs and index funds like those that mirror the S&P 500 can expose investors to the stock market for fees as low as 0.04 percent. (That is just four one-hundredths of one percent!) That's as close to free as one can get! It's easy to learn about ETFs and index funds. Many discount brokers provide easy-to-use educational materials at no cost. Some of these resources are in video format, so anyone can just watch and learn. Today it is so simple to get helpful information; there is no reason to be confused. I will provide a list of resource materials in the Appendix at the end of this book.

It would be impossible and irresponsible of me to advise specific ETFs or index funds. That would require a complete understanding of your age, time horizon, risk tolerance, and many other financial particulars. That is not the point of this book. I am not a certified financial planner, and even they cannot advise anyone without first knowing all their particulars. The point of this book is to share with my family and friends what I have learned the hard way over the

last 40 years. I have learned that many managed portfolios do not beat, or even match, the S&P 500. I have
learned that I can buy an index fund or ETF which,
over time, will do as well, or better, than an actively
managed account. I can do this for a ridiculously low
cost. (Cost are also called *expense ratios.*) The money
I would have paid out in fees is left in my accounts
to grow and compound for many years. (Remember,
once fees are taken out of an account, they are gone
for good.) Everyone in this game plays for keeps.

I have studied every aspect of the stock market
for years. When I invest, I analyze balance sheets,
income statements, cash flow statements, and most
of the SEC (Security & Exchange Commission)
reports about the company I am interested in. I analyze reports like the 10 -K, 10- Q, 144/A, S–1, and
8-K. I listen to corporate conference calls, read all
special reports on the company's activities, and study
the critical ratios. Financial ratios help me analyze a
company's valuation, liquidity, profitability, management, efficiency, and growth rate. I also perform discounted future cash flow analyses for companies in
which I plan to invest.

Believe me; I'm not telling you all of this to convince you how smart I am. *Quite the opposite.* I have
spent hundreds of hours on analysis and thousands
of dollars on research, and guess what ... my investments almost *never* beat the returns of the S&P 500

index; and what's worse is, neither do most investors, including the pros.

Even hedge funds with genius mathematical quantifiers and options traders can't consistently beat the returns of the S&P 500.

Do you see where I'm going with all this? There are very few people in this world that have been fortunate enough to consistently beat returns that can be achieved by simply investing in the overall market. I'm trying to convey some of the things that I had to learn the hard way. It would take years to develop the expertise that I have in equity analysis, and you still won't likely be able to do any better than buying low-cost index funds or ETFs, and holding them for long periods of time. Don't get me wrong, I don't regret the education I've gained, but I

EYE OPENER

I have spent hundreds of hours on analysis and thousands of dollars on research, and guess what...my investments almost never beat the returns of the S&P 500 index, and neither do most investors: including the pros.

realize that for the most part, it is unnecessary to have that level of understanding to succeed in the stock market. You can do as well, or better than me, and better than most mutual funds, by simply understanding what is written in this single chapter, and doing things the easy and inexpensive way.

As an investor, and serious student of the financial markets, it is only natural that I have financial heroes that I regard as exceptional. One of the heroes that I look up to is Warren Buffett.[3] He is arguably one of the greatest investors of all time. Warren is the Director of Berkshire Hathaway. He recently made a bet in 2008. The bet was for one million dollars, with the proceeds going to the winner's charity of choice.

Let me tell you a little bit about that bet. **Warren bet that over a 10-year period, starting in 2008, a low-cost S&P 500 index fund could out-perform hedge funds selected by a famous New York City-based**

Warren Buffett's bet that the S&P 500 Index could outperform hedge funds, should be a real wake up call to all investors.

---

3 Warren E. Buffett is the Director of Berkshire Hathaway. He is also the largest shareholder. Warren is considered one of the greatest investors in the world. He is also a philanthropist, pledging to give away most of his billions.

money manager, Protégé Partners. Warren chose the Vanguard S&P 500 index fund: **VFINX.** The money manager would select five funds of hedge funds and hope to outperform the S&P 500. These hedge funds would no doubt involve some of the most brilliant minds in the financial world today.

Would you like to know the results after eight years? Well here it is:

The S&P 500 index fund is up 65.67%
Hedge funds are up 21.87%

If this were a boxing match, the referee would probably stop the fight.

But, as they say in the television infomercials: *wait there's more!*

Warren Buffett has offered the following advice to the trustees of his estate in the event of his death. He would like his estate to be invested in the following manner: 10% of the funds should be in short-term U.S. Treasuries, *and 90% of the funds should be in an S&P 500 index. Did I mention the fact that we're talking about one of the greatest investors and richest persons on earth?* Warren is a man who has access to billions of dollars, and unlimited amounts of financial research. Despite all that, he is determined that the absolute best place for the money that his heirs will receive would be with a **low expense ratio** *S&P 500-index fund. (He suggested Vanguard, but there are many to choose from,)*

Possibly one of the most important things anyone can do while reading this book is to re-read the paragraph printed above. Re-read it slowly, and let that information sink in.

I know, as I reflect on 40 years of investing, that Buffet's advice would have done wonders for me. It would have saved me a great deal of suffering. I could have just bought some super low-cost index funds and let my fortunes rise with the market. Even though there have been multiple corrections and recessions, I would have done very well indeed, thank you. Instead, I bought and sold individual stocks. I won some, lost some, and aggravated myself to a degree that I cannot even explain. I was 100% positive that I could do better than a boring old index fund. **I was wrong!** The S&P 500 Index fund knocked my socks off year after year. I would be hundreds of thousands of dollars ahead of the game today if I just bought index funds and left them alone. May I make my confession now? I was an idiot! I thought I could beat the market and the millions of brilliant people who were competing against me. I thought my money was somehow magical, and the stocks I bought would simply go up and make me rich. I knew how to read balance sheets, cash flow statements, and income statements. I thought that was going to make me special. Well, it didn't. I almost NEVER beat the returns of the S&P 500 index. **Finally, it dawned on me!** When it dawned on me, I did the following:

I put my upturned hands out in front of me. I slowly lowered my head into the palms of my hands, and said the following words: "STUPID ... STUPID ... STUPID!" That was it. That was my epiphany; my light bulb moment. I berated myself most unmercifully, telling myself I was an idiot, nitwit, numbskull, etc. ... fill in the blanks. I re-read the wisdom of John Bogle[4]. I finally got it! I titrated out of many of my stock positions (not all), and bought index funds with the proceeds. My investment performance has been much better ever since. I had a slow and painful learning curve, and that cost me a lot of time and money.

I don't want my children to have to go through that. I want them to be successful. I want them to be able to retire with a substantial pension fund that will make their golden years sweet. This is the advice I give to my adult sons, and their wives. *The fact is, I wrote this book* for the benefit of my family. Since I had to print it up anyway, I thought I would share it with you. If my adult children read it, understand it, and share it with their children, I have done my job, and consider it a major success! I expect that many others who read it will someday be millionaires. I hope you will be one of them.

The magic that makes all of this happen is *time*. The more time an investor has before retirement, the greater the likelihood of accumulating an

---

4 John C. Bogle is the founder of Vanguard Mutual Funds. He developed the first index fund, and has been a strong advocate of individual investors. He is a prolific writer, and has educated millions of investors on how to invest without incurring heavy expenses.

enormous nest egg. Investing is not nearly as complicated as many would like to have you believe. In fact, it's one of the simplest things that a person can do. *Start your investments as early as possible because time is a critical piece of the investment equation.*

Have you ever heard of the Rule of 72? Let me explain: it's quite easy. When we divide the number 72 by the return we expect to make, the quotient is the number of years that it will take for the investment to double. Let's use a very simple example: Earning 10% annually, money will double in 7.2 years. Just to make the math a bit easier, let's call it seven years. (That will require 10.29%. This rule is a quick calculator and is not exact to the penny.) Let's start the math. Mary has $10,000 at age 22. If she earns 10.29% on her investments, she will have $20,000 at age 29. At age 36 she will have $40,000, and at age 43 she will be up to $80,000. By age 50, Mary has $160,000. At age 57, she has $320,000. By the time Mary is 64, she has $640,000. Now think about that for a moment. Mary has $640,000, and she hasn't even added a single penny to the original $10,000. By the way, if Mary doesn't need the money, and she hold on another 7 years, she will be looking at 1.28 million!! Mary will only be 73, and if she is still in good health, she may want to take several luxury cruises every year. She sure won't have to worry about having the money! (These calculations assume no taxes or expenses) Mary put in the first $10,000 dollars, and the market put in hundreds of thousands more! That's the way this is supposed to work!

My point here is to show the value of time and compounding. Time is the key element that makes all this compounding work. Do not get sidetracked by the enormity of financial blather that has become ubiquitous in every media format. If you want to get wealthy, it takes time. Sorry, none of this is sexy. When you're 22, the very last thing you want to think about is being 64; I get it. One of my great regrets in life is I did not know the power of compounding when I was 22. I still did not know it at age 32. I did not learn this until my time window had already deteriorated. I was just a working stiff, but I could have retired a multimillionaire if I knew then what I know now. It simply is not that difficult. If you are reading these words, and you are under 30 years old, please take them to heart and begin to invest now. Do not wait until you have "a little extra cash." Believe me, that day will never come, and you will squander away the critical years that could be building a fortune. Regardless of your age, the very best time to start investing is RIGHT NOW!

So, we were talking about some of my financial heroes. I could not possibly continue this book without mentioning the name, John C. Bogle. He is truly a pioneer and a giant in the investment world. Let me tell you a little bit about him. John Bogle is the founder of the Vanguard Group. He founded that company in 1974. It is now the largest mutual fund and index fund company in the world, with assets in excess of $2 trillion. Even Warren Buffett, one of the world's richest men and greatest investor, wants the bulk of his estate to be invested in the Vanguard S&P 500 index fund after his death. Mr. Bogle has written numerous books, many of which I have read, and would recommend to you. He is a firm believer in the concept of mutual funds and index funds. He is also an advocate of very low expense ratios, so that the investor reaps and keeps most of the gains. I like and agree with the advice Mr. Bogle provides. If you follow his advice, your fortunes should grow nicely. I encourage you to start with Mr. Bogle's book: **The Little Book of Common Sense Investing: The Only Way to Guarantee Your Fair Share of Stock Market Returns.**

I have a comprehensive financial library, but if I had to pare it down to just a few books, I would certainly include those written by John Bogle. I say this even though Mr. Bogle has essentially confirmed that much of the effort that I expended in my investment career was largely a waste of time. If I did as he instructed, I could have achieved results far better than those that I did through great effort, expense, and aggravation. He has essentially said that I did not have to expend the thousands of hours I did on research. The good news is that Mr. Bogle will teach you how to be a superior investor with almost no effort. It is no surprise that Fortune Magazine designated him as one of the investment industries giants of the 20th century. In addition to being a financial powerhouse, Mr. Bogle is also a fine man, a wonderful human being, and someone who understands what the real values in life truly are. Put this book on the top of your "must read list". If you don't want to spend the money to purchase his books, most public libraries have copies for you to borrow.(He is extremely rich so he won't mind that you didn't buy a copy. He is a good man and truly wants everyone to be succesful.) Make a point of reading John Bogle; you will not be sorry.

Summary:
Investing is not all that complicated. You *can* make it extremely complicated, as I did, and still not do any better than simply investing in an S&P 500 index fund, and/or other index funds that represent large segments of the stock market. The magic that makes everything work is *time*. We reviewed the Rule of 72, and understanding this simple concept will help in understanding how important time and return rates are to reaching investment goals.

We talked a bit about Warren Buffett and John Bogle, two of the true giants of the financial industry. Both of these guys are in their 80s, and I still find every word they say fascinating and extremely pertinent. Warren Buffett is one of the richest men on earth, and arguably one of the greatest investors in the world, and has decided that his heirs should invest most of their inheritance in one of the wonderful S&P 500 index funds in Mr. Bogle's Vanguard. This fact alone should tell you a lot. If it's good enough for Warren Buffett, the world's greatest investor, it's good enough for me!

It's time now to go to chapter 3 where we will discuss the *100% guarantee*. Not very many things come with a 100% guarantee, especially with regard to investing. But in chapter 3, I will present something that is absolutely, positively guaranteed 100%. **This guarantee is extremely important to know.** See you there.

CHAPTER 3

The 100% Guarantee

Very few things in life come with a 100% guarantee. This is especially true when talking about investments, but here is something that I can guarantee with absolutely no doubt of being wrong. I can give the guarantee in writing, that's how sure I am of it. It is critically important that this guarantee be understood for reasons I will explain shortly.

Before I provide the guarantee, consider this:

During the last 100 years, the S&P 500 has been through depressions, recessions, panics, bear markets, wars, and some downright awful declines. Despite all that, $10,000 invested in 1917 would be worth over 46 million dollars today: $46,380,633.09.

Now, are you ready? Here it is; the **100%** **Guarantee:**

While I believe the stock market is one of the best ways to build wealth, if you invest in the stock market long term, sometime during your investment life, I guarantee you will lose money. That's right: I can guarantee that the value of your investments will at some point go down. You will have an hour, a day, a week, or even a year or more when your investments are worth less than they were earlier. This will happen. There is no chance that the value of your equities will never go down. Money invested in stocks will fluctuate in value.

It is critically important that you understand this concept because it is perfectly normal, and I never want you to panic when it happens. Just as we know that not every day will be perfect weather, we must understand that financial markets are not always sunny. The markets experience financial rain, wind, storms, and even hurricanes. These will come, I assure you. Your little nest egg will get battered about. Please do not panic. From time to time, the amount of money in your account will go down. The price of a stock, or even a basket of stocks in a mutual fund, index fund, or ETF, can go up and down with supply and demand, economic vitality, and even catastrophic events. Before any investment journey begins, you must understand and accept this reality. Hundreds of billions of dollars have been lost for no reason other than investors panic and sell out of their positions at the most inappropriate time. I know you think that *you* will never do that. *You* have every confidence of staying "cool" during the most difficult periods. Believe me, when the markets go bad, you may not feel the same way. Markets can sink and sink badly. The talking heads on TV can whip up investors into a frenzy with commentary like this: *"This market has just made a new low, and if it breaks the 200-day moving average, it could sink much more. When will the bleeding stop? When will this declining market hit bottom? Are we entering a bear market? What should investors do now? Up next ... an expert who says that the market will sink another 20%!"*

Before we know it, we get sucked into the vortex, wringing our hands, and telling ourselves:

"Everything we had will soon be gone! The only hope now is to get out with something!" Doom... Gloom ... then Zoom ... we start to do stupid things. Stupid things that will probably wind up costing us money.

This is when full-service brokers earn their keep. They can talk their clients off the window ledge. These brokers know what I'm about to tell you now: **Things will get better.** One of the broker's jobs is to calm the fear and walk investors off from the ledge of the building so that no one jumps. My job is to keep you from ever walking out onto the ledge in the first place. I'm telling you in advance that these times will come; in fact, I guarantee that they will come. **It's no big deal.** These times can even be leveraged by taking advantage of the situation, and purchasing more equities at bargain prices. Fear often drives the market down much further than the fundamental financials justify. These situations could be wonderful buying opportunities. If you know in advance that these periods of decline will come, you are girded against panic. You know that these cycles of falling prices will end, and periods of great returns will likely wash away all those losses, and then propel your portfolio on to even higher highs. You can relax when the inevitable occurs because you know it's coming, you expect it, and you simply yawn when others fret and panic.

Self-talk is a powerful concept that every investor must understand fully. In fact, it is a concept that applies to many situations in life. Self-talk can, and often does, lead to action. If the self-talk is irrational, it will lead to irrational action. If it is rational and logical, it will lead to rational actions. People can use self-talk to scare themselves to death, or to be motivated into action. Self-talk can focus the mind or send it spinning out of control. Once irrational emotions influence investment decisions, things do not generally end well.

Let me share some of the self-talk that causes the unsophisticated investor to sell low and lock in painful losses. These are the little

SELF-TALK

Self-talk is that internal dialog that we have with ourselves. It can be rational or irrational. When it is rational, it is a tremendous help, and can prevent us from making big mistakes. When irrational, it is as damaging as a tornado. We can talk ourselves into doing things that are beyond stupid.

messages that people tell themselves. They are dangerous little internal dialogs that have cost investors billions.

"Oh, my goodness, I'm going to lose everything! I had better sell now and at least get some of my money back."

"This is the end! Nothing like this has ever happened before, and it will end in devastation. I'll go broke for sure!"

"The market will never recover." "This could be another 1929 type depression!"

"Everything is hopeless; the recession will wipe everyone out, I'll be left penniless!"

"What have I done! I knew I should never have invested my money in stocks. Why did I do it? How could I have been so stupid?"

"I made a huge mistake! The only smart thing is to get out while I still have something left."

"There is nothing but bad news and terrible earnings reports. When the second shoe drops, I'll lose a fortune".

These are all very dramatic statements, and they are usually **wrong**. These are the kinds of statements that investors must not make to themselves. They are the kinds of self-statements that could make us lose all confidence. When investors tell themselves this stuff, they start to unravel. They start to head for the window ledge. They tell themselves it's time to jump;(sell.) Jumping and selling are the same things in my book. Either way, you get crushed. (I'm being melodramatic here... don't ever jump!)

This stuff happens all the time. That's why I gave you the guarantee. You know it's going to happen, it's going to happen over and over, and it's no big deal. Yes, your portfolio value will at some point go down. Yes, it will be depressing and demoralizing. Yes, it may start to feel hopeless and painful. These feeling are quite normal. This is the time to keep your big boy pants on. I told you to expect losses if you want to be an investor. Volatility, value fluctuation, up, downs, and sideways, are part of the game. Being able to take it is a pre-requisite to being an investor. When you step into the boxing ring, expect a few punches will come your way. It will not always be easy, and it will not always be fun. We are on a ship to the land of milk and honey; but like any ocean voyage, there may be rough seas. The objective is to hold the course. Steady as she goes. Don't jump ship! When storms pass, we will keep getting closer to that safe and happy shore where *we won't have to work no more!* (Critical Mass)

It is always a good idea to leave a portion of the portfolio in liquid assets. Cash on hand will enable an investor to take advantage of unrealistically low prices. Even more importantly, when the portfolio is needed to provide income, investors never want to be in a position to have to sell equities when they are at distressed levels. By maintaining cash in the portfolio, there will be no need to sell equities when the market is down. These concepts are not complicated. It may take some time for a downtrend in the stock market to end before things reverse course. Maintaining a few years' worth of cash provides breathing room for the second and even third year of a down market. If you don't require any money from your investments, then waiting for a recovery is certainly no problem. If looking at your portfolio when it is down troubles you, or makes you anxious, *don't look at it.*

The average return of the S&P 500 since 1928 has been around 10%. Now that doesn't mean that we will make 10% every year, in fact, we may go through periods of time where our losses are in double digits. It is possible to have uncomfortable stretches of time with negative returns. The good thing is; usually, after a stretch of negative returns, there may be multiple years of positive returns which improve the average. In a period of 40-50 years, investors in the S&P 500 index should average about 7%-10% return per year. Did you notice that I said 40 to 50 years? I did not say 40-50 minutes, hours, days, or weeks. Some people find the thought of seeing their savings fluctuate up and down so uncomfortable; they simply refuse to invest in the stock market. That is unfortunate because they will be missing out on a terrific opportunity to enhance wealth. It is imperative that you understand how perfectly normal it is to have fluctuations in the market.

The following statements are the kind of self-talk needed to control fear and panic when the market is collapsing:

(They can save you from making costly emotional mistakes.)

"Wow, the market is way down, and it looks like it may stay that way for a while. Fortunately, I know that in the long run, I'll probably earn 7% - 10%, even considering this particularly crappy time in the market."

"Oh well, I'm sure not happy about this down market, but I know I've been guaranteed that I will lose money from time to time, and this is one of those times. This type of thing happens regularly, but I know that markets eventually move higher over time, so it's no big deal."

"I am certainly not going to sell, and I'm not smart enough to time the top or bottom of any market. History has shown that corrections and bear markets eventually come to an end and recoveries proceed from them."

"Oh well, I'm not happy about this downtrend, but it won't have any impact on my day to day finances, or what I do this weekend."

"It bugs me to watch my portfolio value go down from day to day. Maybe I'll take a vacation from looking at my portfolio. I'm not going to make any changes, so why should I aggravate myself by looking at it every few

hours? I was told that this would happen, and now here it is. I was also told not to panic, so I won't."

"Oh well ... It may be a while before I get back to where I was. The good thing is, my dividends are buying more shares cheap while the market is down. When things recover, all those extra shares should be a big help moving my portfolio higher."

Do you see the dramatic difference between the two types of self-talk that I've displayed? The first series of self-statements are full of doom and gloom. Those statements often lead to an investor selling out her positions when prices are low. Panic selling can lock in big losses that are difficult to recover from. Even if the market continues to go down, the investor who sold out at low prices should not pat himself or herself on the back. It could take years to recover from the losses that have been locked in by selling at depressed prices. Ask anyone who sold out during one of the severe downturns how they felt about it after the market fully recovered and moved higher. It is a very sick feeling when you watch a position you sold in panic, recover to where it was, then zoom up 35% higher without you! If you sold at a 25% loss, and then missed out on the 35% gain; your total loss is 60%! (I know because I have done just that!).

It astounds me to see how much psychology is involved with investing. Here is one thing that amazes me, especially with new investors. An investor finally decides that he or she will put some money in the market. The assumption is that the market will somehow know that this is their money. That means it is special money. It is money that they had to work hard to earn and be very conservative to save. Now that the market has this special money, the assumption is that only good things will happen to their very special money. The money will grow of course, and nothing bad will ever happen to it. It will be treated by the market as the very precious, special, and unique money that it is. So far, that's a wonderful fantasy, *but it's a fantasy that is entirely wrong.* The market doesn't care about your money, and I can guarantee that your money will have bad things happen to it eventually. You simply must be prepared and know how to react when that happens.

Let me give you an analogy. Let's say that someone watches a horror movie, and the first time they see it, their fear is real and palpable. Let's say that same person watches the movie a few more times. The very things that made the moviegoer jump with fear the first time he saw it, will most likely leave him nonplussed by the fourth or fifth time. He knows what's coming, it's no shock, and he knows the results. This is exactly what I'm talking about when I give you the *guarantee.* You know that the market will eventually turn down and that the value of your portfolio will reflect that drop. You also know, that over the long haul; and by long haul I mean 10, 15,

20, or more years; that drop will be inconsequential. The fear is gone. If you need to pay someone a percentage of your portfolio's value to hold your hand, and tell you this from time to time, then go ahead. I just don't think it's necessary, and I think it's a very expensive piece of psychological support that I'm trying to provide right here for free.

Folks like Warren Buffett embrace these downturns in the market with great enthusiasm. He teaches that he has made monumental sums by buying when the market is rattled with fear. His famous saying is: "Be fearful when others are greedy, and greedy when others are fearful." I would give those words some serious consideration if I were you, considering this: **If you had invested $1000 in Warren Buffett's Berkshire Hathaway fund in 1964, by 2017 that $1000 would be worth $13 million! Believe me, between the years 1964 and 2017 there were many very depressing down years in the market. That didn't prevent Warren Buffett from turning $1000 into over $13 million. Think about that when you see frightened investors out on the ledge. Don't be one of them.**

Summary:
There are not many guarantees when it comes to investing. The one guarantee that is unequivocal

is the fact that at some point during your investing career your equity portfolio will fluctuate in value. It will go up, and it will go down. Investment portfolios can even go below the original sum they started with. It is critically important to know all of this up front. When we know this up front, and we expect these things to happen, we won't panic when they do. It is panic, and the sense of urgency that makes investors do the exact opposite of what they should do. They sell at the low point, thinking that is the only way they can preserve their capital.

The correct thing is to not panic. Investors should consider taking advantage of the big stock sale and buy more shares cheaply. That's exactly what Warren Buffett does. The fact that he turned $1,000 in 1964 into $13 million in 2017 is a pretty good example of how well that works. The old saying: "being forewarned is being forearmed," is very true when it comes to investing. I'm telling you in advance that your investments will fluctuate, and you will most certainly experience losses at some point in your tenure. (Warren Buffet did on his way to turning $1,000 into $13,000,000.) These losses are a fact of investing life. They will come as surely as the rain. There is no way they can be avoided in a portfolio of stock-based investments. You now know that you will experience some losses, so it will not be a shock when it happens. Because these losses are expected and anticipated, the wise investors are prepared for them, and will not be inclined to sell at the absolute worst time. We should embrace market declines like a child embraces a snowstorm ... a time for excitement and opportunity.

CHAPTER 4
Risk

There are a number of ways to deal with risk. We can avoid it, mitigate it, transfer it, or ignore it. Everything we do in life has some risk. Walking across a street, riding in a car, playing a game of basketball. We accept these risks and calculate the likelihood of injury seamlessly and naturally.

When it comes to investing our money, our financial risk analysis is not as natural and seamless as is our survival risk analysis.

First, we must understand that when we invest our money, we are putting it at risk. Even the money in our pocket is at risk. Someone could rob us, or we could lose it. There is always some element of risk with our valuables. Even very safe U.S. Treasury bonds can go down in value. Let me provide an example. Let's say an investor buys a $10,000 treasury bond that has a 10-year maturity and pays 2.4%. About three years later, the new 10-year Treasury bond is paying 4.8%. No one in their right mind is going to want to buy the bond that pays only 2.4% when they can get twice as much on a new bond. If the bond owner must sell his bond, someone *will* buy it, but they will buy it at a *deep discount,* and he will not receive his original amount of principal.

Blue chip, conservative, dividend-paying stocks can also go down in value. There is no avoiding some risk. As a rule, the more risk we accept, the higher return we expect. Unfortunately, that is not always the case. Even if all the fundamentals of our investments are perfect, the market itself could become volatile. Catastrophic events can send a market plummeting. When we make an investment, we are accepting all the risks that come with that investment and with the market environment.

Well, you say, there is no risk if I just put my money in a bank account. There is no way I can lose by being in cash.

Yes, there is. You may not make enough from the bank to offset inflation. That makes your money worth less every year. If you lock money into a long-term low-return commitment, like a bank CD, you may have "opportunity risk". That is, you may miss out on opportunities that could have made many times more than having your money stuck in the "safe bet". When it comes to money, you are always accepting risk.

Have you ever watched nature shows on cable TV? I enjoy those shows immensely, especially the ones filmed in Africa. I am partial to the big cats, like lions. The lion is the king of the beasts and the top of the food chain. Lions can teach us a lot about risk. In fact, we can learn about risk by observing every animal and insect in nature. All creatures must be risk analysts. For them, it's a matter of life and death. If a creature attempts to make a meal out of something that could kill, maim, or disable it, that creature might have a very short life indeed. In most cases, an error in calculating risk ends up with that creature being killed and eaten by another. In nature, there is no safety net. A broken leg, a severe wound, or a shattered jaw will pretty much guarantee a slow and painful death, followed by being devoured by scavengers. Nature plays for keeps, and the stakes are high.

Getting back to lions: A lion knows that if it receives a kick in the jaw by a powerful antelope or zebra, it might as well be dead. A broken jaw and damaged teeth will make it impossible to hunt or eat. The lion will die a slow and indignant death. The lion mitigates its risk by choosing prey carefully. To reduce risk, the lion prefers the old, the young, the weak, the injured, or the isolated. A lion analyzes the risk before attacking. While a big powerful male antelope would provide a fabulous feast, it may not be worth the risk. These animals are dangerous, and have fatally injured lions. The lion uses patience to wait for the right opportunity. A female lion might have cubs to feed. If she gets injured or killed, her cubs will die. She watches the herd, studies the individuals in it, and waits for an investment (I mean animal), that is just what she is looking for. She wants one that will provide nice returns for the effort invested, and one that will not likely hurt or kill her. She knows that her life and the lives of her babies depend on sound risk management. First, she selects her target, then she calculates the risk of attacking it. Once she determines the reward is worth the risk, she strikes!

Investors can learn something about risk from lions.

RISK ANALYSIS

All living creatures are risk analysts. That's why they are still living! It is when risk is ignored or miscalculated, that a creature meets his death.

Even the king of the beasts must consider risk. Lions do not take unreasonable chances. They watch and wait until the risk is low and the reward almost guaranteed. Never forget that when you wander into the jungle of stock investing. Hungry predators are waiting for you to make a wrong move so that they can devour your capital. Always minimize your risks.

A highly speculative stock is to the investor what a big, powerful male antelope is to the lion. The large, muscular antelope will be a tremendous feast if the lion's attack is successful. (Big risk / big reward.) If something goes wrong, if the antelope lands a powerful kick, the lion can be severely disabled. Not only will she have lost her meal, and the meat her cubs need, but, because of her injury, she has put future opportunities at risk. Her future and her cub's futures are now in trouble. Investors have a similar problem when they suffer a major loss on a bad stock. The investor has not only lost money, she has done damage to future earnings because her principal has been diminished.

A safer bet for the lion would be to attack a young, injured, or old animal that would provide meat without much risk. To the investor, boring old S&P 500 index funds provide returns with less risk. The likelihood of a deadly blow to the portfolio is much less than it would be if the money were all in a single stock.

For the lion, this is a life or death decision. The investor should take her risks just as seriously. Don't ever think for a moment that other investors will not happily devour you if you make a mistake. Stock picking can be a very unforgiving game. That stock you are so anxious to buy is the very one some other investor has decided it is now time to sell. One of you is right, and one is wrong. Ask investors who owned Tyco[5] or Enron[6] when things went terribly bad. Fortunes were lost on those two stocks alone. Be skeptical, be cautious, and be informed before you commit your money. Nature and markets play for keeps. Neither will show mercy. Neither will forgive mistakes. Just as the mother lion's cubs will wither and die if she is killed by a bad decision, your family will be deprived of what you will lose by making bad financial decisions.

Animals know instinctively when it makes more sense to flee rather than attack. Their lives depend on winning the risk management game. The problem with investing is simple. Our primal instincts work well if we are under a physical threat. Our adrenaline kicks in, giving us the boost we need to fight or flee. Our instincts are not so effective when it comes to investments. We simply overestimate how keenly we recognize investment hazards. We mistake our feelings for facts. Our instincts warn us to stay clear of a rattlesnake, but not from a questionable stock. When you begin to believe that you "know in your gut," something is a good or bad investment, you are

---

5 Tyco's CEO was indicted on fraud, sending the stock in a downward spiral.

6 Enron stock sunk from $90.56 to just pennies. It filed for one of the largest bankruptcies in U.S. history.

in a dangerous place. Your gut and your instincts are not good barometers of investment risk. While our instincts may save us from life-threatening dangers, they do little to protect us from stupid investments. **When you think you "know" what the market will do tomorrow, you are ripe and ready to be plucked.**

When an investor takes a large position in a single stock, he has chosen to strike the big game. Many things could happen to cause that stock to collapse. One or two bad earnings reports, negative press, corporate scandal, SEC investigations, legal issues, or any one of a number of things could send the stock south. Let's say the stock cost $55 per share, and it drops to $30. That investor just lost nearly half his money, and it could be a very long time before it comes back, if it ever comes back. By the way, investing in individual stocks without a solid understanding of equity analysis is kind of like a mouse chasing a fox. It is very unlikely that there will be a happy ending for the mouse.

Just as individual stocks concentrate risk, mutual funds dilute or diversify risk. Let's say that rather than owning an individual stock, you instead own the S&P 500 index. Within that large basket of stocks, some will do well while others will do poorly. On average though, your results will be up in a rising market, and down in a declining market. That is not true with an individual stock. A stock may go up or down regardless of which direction the market is moving. Index funds and mutual funds dilute the risk of individual stocks. All your eggs are in one gigantic basket, where the breakage of one single egg will not destroy the entire basket.

I was convinced that I could select a few very special eggs to put in my basket. After all, I knew how to analyze stocks, read all the financial data, and do the research necessary to make the right choices. I was willing to accept a higher level of risk and anticipated a much higher return. That is not how it worked out. Some years the S&P 500 index would gain 9% or 10%, but my investments would return 4% or 5%. I always had an excuse. One or two of my positions would suffer unforeseen losses, and skew the entire return downward. It was never my fault of course. "Doooh!!Stupid Market!!" as Homer Simpson might say. I was quite certain that the next year would be completely different. In most cases, it was not. Some unforeseen snafu always clipped one or two of my positions. Sometimes my stocks just didn't do as well as the rest of the market. I gradually began investing in index funds and my results improved dramatically. I still hold some individual stocks, but nowhere near as many as I used to. Watching index funds grow in your portfolio is boring. It couldn't be much more unexciting. But your investments really shouldn't be terribly exciting. They should be secure and steady.

I must admit, that despite the risk, I find investing in a few individual companies invigorating. I do it with a very small percentage of my overall portfolio, and I do not invest unless I have run the company through my equity analysis process. I guess I just enjoy the hunt.

When my doctor told me that I needed a CPAP machine, I researched the companies that manufacture CPAP machines. (CPAP machines are positive pressure devices that people with sleep apnea use to prevent dangerous lapses in breathing during sleep.) I selected the one company with the very best balance sheet and income statement. I did not buy it right away, but the next time I spoke to my doctor, he said very matter-of-factly that "everyone" is on CPAP today, even children. When I continued my research into the company I had chosen, I found that, in fact, their sales were rising every quarter. I hesitated no longer and took a position in that stock. In a very short time, I had made a substantial profit. That stock continues to provide me with dividends and capital gains every year. My wife needed a knee replacement and asked me to investigate the company that manufactured her new knee. Her doctor said that knee replacements were becoming commonplace. We purchased stock of the company that made her new knee, and had wonderful results. Investing in these and other individual companies is a much riskier proposition than investing in index funds. I am still willing to do it because I find the process exciting and invigorating, but I only do it with a tiny part of my portfolio.

When thinking about risk, one should think about the big picture. If the specific reason for your investments is your financial security in retirement, then there is little room for extra risk. Your future and your retirement are much too important to take chances with. Losses are much harder to make up as the years march onward.

Consider this: An investor retires with $1 million, and expects that $1 million to provide an income for the rest of his or her life. Most financial advisors will explain that a withdrawal of 4% per year is about all that should be taken from the portfolio. The money will last 25 years even if it earns nothing. If the portfolio remains invested conservatively, and earns 4%-6% per year, it is most likely that you will **never run out of money,** and in fact, there will be money left over for your heirs. Of course, you can adjust your withdrawal rate, as long as you understand how it will likely affect the longevity of the fund. Another thing to consider is inflation. As long as the fund balance is invested and earning 4%-6% yearly, there will be some room for you to help off-set the increased cost of living brought on by inflation.

By the way, it is very easy to make specific calculations for your individual situation. There are dozens of free financial calculators on the Internet. One calculator I like and recommend can be found at: www.investor.gov. When you get there, go to: *financial planning tools*. Select the calculator required. This site also provides a social security estimator, retirement estimator, and even a mutual fund analyzer. (This is a wonderful site and one you should bookmark and use regularly.)

To use the calculators, simply plug in the numbers, and the calculators will do all the math. Once the results are given, you can tweak the input numbers to see how they change the end results. For instance, plug in the amount currently in your portfolio, enter the amount that is added monthly, and enter an interest rate that the portfolio is reasonably expected to return. Be sure to plug in the number of years that you expect before retirement. Once the 'calculate' button it hit, an answer will appear. In many cases, a similar calculator is available right on your discount brokerage site. Another option is to visit a full-service broker, or a fee-only fiduciary, and ask them to evaluate your situation. Most of these professionals will be happy to do that for you. It is important to have some idea how much money you'll need and how long it will take to accumulate that amount. Some people put this off because they find it depressing and discouraging. Do not make that mistake.

One of the biggest risks that most people are exposed to right now is not having enough money to retire on. That is one risk that must be mitigated, and the earlier, the better. Think of retirement as a three-legged stool. One leg is social security, one leg is a retirement account or pension, and the other leg is cash and real estate. These three legs make for a solid stool.

RETIREMENT RISK

One of the biggest risks people are exposed to is not having enough money to retire on.

Take any one away, and things could be wobbly. By the way, don't panic about Social Security. Social Security is not going anywhere. It will be there when you retire, even if it requires you to wait a tiny bit longer. I would estimate that the risk of Social Security going away is almost zero. By far the much bigger risk is that you are not putting away enough money right now. Don't worry about Social Security; worry about your retirement account. Remember, time is the secret sauce that makes all this stuff work. Wasting time is one of the riskiest investment strategies anyone can engage in!

Many years ago, the retirement risk was often transferred to the employer. When someone got a job, one of the benefits might be the promise of a nice pension in 30-40 years. The employer contributed to a pension account, so at the end of 30 or 40 years, enough money would be there to supply a retiree with a fixed income. For many working people, employer-funded pensions are gone and replaced with a self-contributory program. You should determine if you are one of those people who has to fund their own retirement. Do you work for a company or government agency where a retirement plan is funded or partially funded? Do you work in private industry, or for an organization that provides a contributory retirement plan? Does your company match part of your contribution, and what is the formula? Are you doing everything right to maximize what you can contribute? These are very critical questions that must be asked and answered to mitigate retirement risk. Never assume anything when it comes to your retirement program. If professional help is needed sorting all of this out, get it. Even if it means paying someone to help understand all of this, do it, because getting everything right early in the game is critical.

Many employers offer matching plans, where they will match all or some of the amount that the employee invests in the company-sponsored retirement plan. *Maximize this opportunity.* Let me repeat that: maximize this opportunity. Regardless of whether or not the employer kicks in, a working person should not let a single week go by without adding something to a retirement account

When people think of risk, they often think that risk means doing something that can cause injury or loss, and in many cases, that is true. Believe me, some of life's most dangerous risks involve **NOT DOING** something. *Not* wearing a seatbelt, *not* using PPE (personal protective equipment), and *not* being prepared for the inevitable time when you will not be working.

Not taking a risk is often the riskiest thing a person can do. People who do not invest because they are anxious or afraid of investing in the equity markets, or because they hate the thought of their savings fluctuating in value, may be leaving huge sums of money on the table. Let me give you an example: Let's say you are in your late 20s or 30s, but you want investments that cannot possibly drop in value. You keep your savings "safe" in a money market, savings bank, or checkbook. People who do this often think they will sleep better knowing that their money is not at risk. *Trust me; you should not be sleeping so soundly.* When the savings bank pays 1%, and inflation is 2%, your buying power is shrinking, not growing.

Here is another thing to consider: A portfolio has $10,000 in it, and the investor contributes $500 additionally each month. If that money is invested in super-safe money market funds paying 1% interest, after 35 years the investor will have $264,127.68. The investor thought he would be able to sleep easier knowing that his money would never fluctuate in value. **I certainly hope he enjoyed his sleep-filled nights because they may have cost him $1,643,042.90.**

If he had invested his money in an S&P 500 index fund, and that fund returned an average of 10%, his total after 35 years would be **$1,907,170.58**. (I readily admit that a 10% return is overly optimistic, but even 7% will result in **$936,187**; that's **$672,000** more than the money market!)

Please look at these numbers carefully, and tell me where the greatest risk is. I think it's a lot riskier to hide money away in a money market fund than to have it invested in the S&P 500 Index.

Constructing a portfolio may require holding some cash, some fixed income indexes, and some stock indexes. Your personal mix, called *asset allocation*, is something that involves thought and planning. A financial professional can help you set up that allocation mix. Once it is set, it does not require expensive financial management. It may necessitate rebalancing from time to time. Many discount brokerage firms have tools on board to help with that. As the years progress, that allocation may have to be tweaked some to reflect your change in risk tolerance. No consideration of investment risk is complete without discussing asset allocation. Asset allocation is simply how a portfolio is divided up so that it is not totally invested in just one segment of the market. That kind of diversification allows part of the portfolio to zig while the other parts zag. The portfolio holds funds that reflect different segments of the financial market. In addition to holding U.S. stock funds, it may also contain exposure to the bond markets, international stocks, money market funds, and possibly even commodities. Asset allocation is the equivalent of a large heavy keel on a sailboat. Although that keel adds weight and drag, it prevents the boat from tipping over in choppy water. Without a substantial keel, the sailboat could not withstand wind or waves. Financial winds and waves can wreak havoc on a portfolio. A portfolio needs diversification to serve as a keel to add stability. The size and weight of your diversification keel is determined by your age, risk tolerance, financial needs, etc. (Built-in tools are available on most discount brokerages sites at no cost.) If you don't feel comfortable on your own, get some professional help with diversification. This is too important to get wrong.

It is so easy and comfortable to ignore the fact that some day you may not want to work. Worse yet, you may reach a point where you are not capable of working. When that time comes, income has to come from somewhere. It doesn't all have to come from one source. Some can come from Social Security, some from a pension if you have one, and some from your investments. *Pretending* that time will never come is risky behavior. The great irony of ironies is that the younger a person is, the greater the risk, because young investors have the most to lose. A very young person is almost guaranteed to be able to accumulate a million dollars or more, simply because of the power of time. Young people who ignore this will possibly miss out on millions! DO NOT TAKE THAT RISK!

Summary:

There are many ways to deal with risk. One of the worst ways is to ignore it. Not thinking about, or not preparing for retirement, are very risky behaviors. Time is the secret sauce that makes investing work. Wasting time by not being invested is a very dangerous business. Procrastination is one of an investor's cardinal sins. As I have stated time and again, investing is not just about money, it is very much about time. Ask anyone who waited too long to start to invest.

If your employer has a retirement plan where they match your contribution, or even partially match your contribution, take full advantage of that plan. Be sure to maximize your contribution so that your employer contributes the most they are willing to put in. Even if your employer does not match anything, you should still participate to the max. The years will tick away with or without a retirement savings plan. There are no do-overs. Not a single paycheck should be taken unless some of it is invested for retirement. If any of this is confusing, or you don't know which low-cost funds are best to meet your goals, get some help. I like fee-only fiduciaries because they must by law put your interests first.

CHAPTER 5

What Exactly Are Mutual Funds, Index Funds, ETFs, Stocks, and Bonds?

Let's take a brief look at some of the most common investment vehicles.

Mutual Funds:

Mutual funds are essentially baskets of investments. These investments can be stocks, bonds, or almost anything of value. When most people think of mutual funds, they usually think of funds that contain stocks. The logic of a mutual fund is brilliant. It allows an investor to buy a collection of stocks, bonds, real estate, etc., and thus be invested in that particular segment of the market with less risk than any one individual member of the mutually similar group. A managed mutual fund may be run by a single manager or a team of managers, who use all their skill and expertise to select what they think are the very best investments for that specific basket. A great deal of research and effort goes into this exercise. As a result, the managed mutual fund charges a significant fee for doing this work. The general concept is: The mutual fund managers are much more sophisticated than we are, and they can select the very best assets to go into a fund. That selection of assets then reflects the underlying objective of the fund they have created. For instance, if the fund is supposed to reflect the healthcare industry, the managers will select stocks for the fund that will all be related to healthcare in some way. Investors can determine what type of funds they want to invest in. If for instance, the investor wants a fund that consists of only dividend-paying stocks, they can purchase one with that objective. Managed funds monitor and change the makeup of the fund as needed. All of this takes time and people to accomplish, so the fund charges an expense fee commensurate with the amount of work involved. This fee is usually stated as an *expense ratio*, and is expressed as a percentage. For instance, an expense ratio of 1.25% means that the fee to manage this fund is 1.25% of the value under management. If an investor owns $10,000 worth of the fund, the yearly cost is $125. At $100,000, the yearly fee jumps to $1,250. Mutual fund fees have a very wide range. They tend to be higher than Index funds, and ETF's. Some specialty mutual funds can have very high fees due to the amount of management required.

The hope is that these managers will be able to beat the returns of a benchmark like the S&P 500. (The S&P 500 is a collection of 500 large company stocks, and generally, reflects the overall U.S. stock market. The S&P 500 is commonly used as a benchmark, or yardstick, against which to measure gains or losses in other investments.) The reality is that most fund managers do not beat the benchmark associated with their fund. Some do, and if you are lucky enough to have selected the mutual fund and the managers that have outperformed the market, you will do very well. Let me restate that: you will do very well for that year. The high-performing mutual funds and the managers that run them may not repeat that winning performance next year. It is not unusual for a mutual fund to perform wonderfully one year and then have a mediocre performance after that. If an investor is very impressed by a stellar performance, then runs out and buys the fund, he might do so just in time for the fund to experience mediocre results. That happens all the time. It is almost comical to watch as financial magazines shout out headlines announcing the very top-performing mutual funds of last year. (The implication of that headline is that now you know the very best mutual funds to buy.) It doesn't matter how many times this technique of choosing funds fails; it remains a great way to sell magazines and excite investors. It is not, however, the best way to choose a fund.

When investing in mutual funds, it is very important that you look at expense ratios. I cannot over-emphasize how important this is. Many mutual funds have expense ratios of 1% or higher. Some mutual funds charge a fee called a *load*, in addition to the management fee. I would avoid those funds. Some companies like Vanguard, Charles Schwab, Ameritrade, E-Trade, and Fidelity offer very good mutual funds with low expense ratios. I personally own some Vanguard and Fidelity mutual funds that have low management fees. These fees are higher than the fees associated with index funds or ETFs, but that is to be expected because they provide active management. I am a stickler about fees. I dislike paying any more than 35 basis points in fees for any investment. A 1% fee is equal to 100 basis points. If you find a mutual fund that has a fee of 35 basis points, that means you are paying 35/100 of one percent. That may not sound like much, but over the course of 10, 20, 30, or more years, it really adds up. I am only willing to pay 35-40 basis points if I am completely convinced that the managers running the fund have done a fabulous job over multiple years, and will likely continue to do so. I have paid fees higher than 35-40 basis points if the fund has an exceptional long-term record of beating the market. I never, ever pay a load, though. (Upfront loads are like a big service charge just to get into the fund.) I have seen loads as high as 6%. Buying a mutual fund with a 6% front-end load would essentially mean that you are only putting 94% of your money to work. Ironically, many of these load funds do no better than their no-load counterparts.

Remember, one reason people invest in mutual funds is that by doing so, they own a basket of stocks or bonds, not just one. That spreads the risk so that if one individual stock or bond goes bankrupt, or fails miserably, it won't destroy the bulk of the investment. Just to cite one example, many people had their entire retirement accounts invested in Enron. When the stock completely collapsed, they were left with nothing.

Of course, buying a mutual fund is like buying a vehicle. You don't walk into a car dealer and say; "give me a vehicle." That would be ridiculous. You need to know what it is you want that vehicle to do for you. Do you need a large luxury car for long trips, an economy car for utility, a sporty muscle car, or an SUV? Maybe you need a truck with a plow. Mutual funds are much the same. Investors must determine what their objective is first. What is it they need the fund to do, and over what time period. Someone in their 20's or 30's will probably want to invest in a mutual fund that provides growth. Investors looking for income, will want a fund that provides steady cashflow. There are many funds that provide a mixture of those things. There are thousands to choose from and lots of places to learn about exactly what will work for you.

Finding good information about mutual funds is very easy to do today. Using the Internet, and all the tools and information available there makes your investing life so much easier. Data that long ago would have taken Warren Buffett all day to find and evaluate is available in just a few keystrokes on a computer! A great deal of that information is available at no cost. If you have an account with a discount broker like Fidelity or Charles Schwab, the research materials that they provide are astounding. If an investor is willing, as I am, to spend a little bit of money on research, there are some very helpful sites that can be subscribed to. (Morningstar.com premium is an example of one that I like very much, and use regularly). I would also encourage all investors to subscribe to AAII. (American Association of Individual Investors).

For someone just getting started, it might be a good idea to hire a fee-only fiduciary, or financial planner. While I don't like paying fees, sometimes it makes sense to have professional guidance help set the proper trajectory. Once you know what you are doing, you should be able to manage your own account.

Examples of mutual funds: *There are thousands to choose from.*

The examples that are listed in the next chart, are just random selections, not recommendations. I do not recommend specific investments.

I simply want to demonstrate how they differ in various categories. Please pay special attention to the *expense ratio* and load if any. When calculated over long periods of time, these expense differences significantly change your end results. *I never pay a load,* although I might be willing to pay a small one-time fee if I must to get a specific fund that I feel strongly about. I always try to find very low expense ratios.

Today, information about mutual funds is easily available from hundreds of sources. Morningstar is a company that rates and evaluates mutual funds, and while I subscribe to Morningstar's premium services, investors can get much of their information for free. I really like Morningstar, and I trust them. Log on free at: morningstar.com.

**Examples of Mutual Funds (From finra.
org / Morningstar 1/31/17)
(Remember, these are not recommendations,
just random selections for you to see.)
Huge amounts of reference materials
are available for free on the Internet, at
libraries, and via brokerage companies.**

Mutual Fund	Ticker	1-year return	5-year return	10-year return	Expense ratio & Load
Dodge & Cox Large Cap Value	DODGX	21.28	17.01	5.93	.52 & 0
Lord Abbott Opportunity Fund	LVOAX	16.39	12.99	8.95	1.17 & 5.75
Valueline	VALIX	2.89	8.33	5.46	1.15 & 0
Vanguard Star Fund Investor Shares	VGSTX	6.55	8.89	5.56	.34 & 0

Please also note that some of the funds I listed as examples have loads. I avoid loads like the plague. I simply refuse to buy a fund where only part of my money gets put to work. Pay very close attention to all the fees and expenses that you are asked to pay.

There are many places to find mutual funds listed, along with their prices. Business papers like

Barron's, The Wall Street Journal, and Investor's Business Daily, list mutual funds, ETF's, and Index Funds. The easiest way to check out a mutual fund is to do it on the Internet. If you know the name or symbol of the fund you are interested in, you can quickly get a quote on line. You can use your brokerage account if you have one. Even if you don't have an account, you can use free and easy to use web sites like:

Yahoo Finance, MSNBC, Google Finance, MSN Money, CNN Money, Market Watch, Kiplinger. Just log on to one of these sites and start a search. In the search box, type in the ticker symbol. *(A ticker symbol is the group of letters that the fund uses to identify itself. An example of a ticker symbol is: FPURX. That is the symbol for Fidelity Puritan Fund.)* If the funds ticker symbol is not known, use the funds the name, or search by the criteria you are interested in. These sites make it very easy to search for funds.

Remember: Mutual funds transactions are priced at the end of the day after the market closes. The price is determined by dividing the net asset value by the number of shares outstanding. You won't know exactly how much you paid for the fund, or how much you sold it for until the fund calculates the NAV (net asset value) at the end of the day.

Investing and researching is a thousand times easier today than in it was in the not too distant past. *(My goodness ... it is getting so easy to get financial information, there is really no excuse for living in the dark!)*

Once the mutual fund is on your screen, study all the information provided. Pay special attention to the *expense ratio*, and any other expenses like *loads* and *12b-1 fees*.[7] (I tend to avoid any funds with 12b-1 fees, loads, or fees above 30-50 basis points.)[8]

In addition to fees, look at what the fund's objective is, as well as its 1-year, 5-year, and 10-year returns history. For homework, here are some mutual funds to practice getting information on. (I am providing the ticker symbols to make it easy.) Look some of these up and practice clicking around on the various data pages. Once you get the hang of it, you may actually enjoy doing the research.

---

7 12b-1 fees are fees are fees charged by the fund for advertising and distribution. Essentially, these fees are marketing expenses that the fund passes on to you.

8 Basis points are expressed as a percentage. For example, 30 basis points is expressed as .30%. That is 30/100ths of one percent.

Some mutual funds to practice doing research:
(These are not recommendations, just examples)

AMPCX	ABALX	CAIBX	CWGIX
AEPGX	ANCFX	GBLAX	AGTHX
AVSX	ANWPX	NEWFX	AWSHX
BSBIX	BERIX	DIAMX	DODBX
DODWX	DODIX	DODFX	DODGX
FBALK	FCNTX	FLVCK	FLPSX
FMILX	FPURX	FTBFX	MQIFX
HACAX	POAGX	VDIGX	VPMCX

Index Funds

Index funds are mutual funds that require little or no management. They invest in the underlying *index* for which they are named or understood to reflect. For example, investors can buy the S&P 500 index, and own all the stocks in the S&P 500. They will not be paying for active management, as there is none. They simply own the index, and their fortunes rise and fall as the index does. We can do the same thing for the Dow Jones, the Russell 2000, or a great variety of other indexes. One of the nice things about index funds is they generally have very low expense ratios. Some of the discount broker index funds are extremely low-cost vehicles.

Ironically, fees for index funds, though low to begin with, have recently been going down even further. The competition among index funds is fierce, so, every year they become a better and better bargain. If that were not good enough, index funds often beat managed mutual funds. Many mutual funds would be very pleased to match the returns of the S&P 500 index. The news about index funds gets even better. Most index funds may be purchased from the fund family on a regular basis without a transaction fee. This allows regular savers to add to their index funds on a weekly or monthly basis. The bottom line is simple. If someone was asked to dream up a nearly perfect way for the average person to invest in the overall market with minuscule expense ratios, that dream come true might be the S&P 500 index fund. (There are other index funds that reflect even broader spectrums of the market. These may contain thousands of companies. Some index funds reflect an entire market segment, like technology, healthcare, etc.)

There are many index funds. Some index funds are much riskier than the average person should consider. Your choice of index funds will be crucial to success. Many retirement portfolios will contain three or four different index funds to spread the risk a little more. For example, a portfolio may contain a large cap index, a small cap index, a medium cap index, and even an international index. Additionally, many portfolios will also contain one or two bond indexes to spread the risk and smooth out returns over time. Once again, an investor's age and risk tolerance are major considerations in determing which funds he or she should choose. I choose my own index funds and purchase them through my discount broker to whom I pay absolutely no management fees. If I must pay nine basis points or 9/100 of one percent, I can live with that. If I am asked to pay 1.3% or 130 basis points for an investment, I'm out. I simply know too well how that amount of expense will diminish my returns. I can assure you that millions of my fellow Americans have no clue of how wide an expense differential there is among funds, and how significant that can be.

It may be a good idea to get some professional financial help when choosing your funds. There are lots of very fine and knowledgeable advisors who can help. If you do decide to pay for some advice, be sure that the person is certified to provide that service. The designation of CFP, (certified financial planner), or CFA, (chartered financial analyst), should assure that the person is qualified to help make sound decisions. A fee-only adviser may also be considered. You will have to pay for that advice, but if the guidance is needed, it could be money well-spent. Amateurs often make very costly and foolish mistakes, and I don't want you to do that. Getting help in the setup phase should put you on the correct trajectory. Once you learn enough to do everything yourself, you won't have to pay for ongoing advice. I am fortunate enough to not require paid advice, but it took me many years of study and experience to get to that place.

I know, most people hate math, but it is important that I explain basis points. Every investor needs to understand the concept of basis points. Failing to understand this will leave an investor woefully ignorant of how to calculate expenses. This is simple stuff, so please take the time to digest it and understand how it works.

A basis point is 1/100th of 1 percent. A hundred basis points is 1 percent. An expense ratio of 0.08 is only eight basis points or 8/100ths of one percent. If we divide 0.08 by 100, it works out to

> **Learn to think in terms of basis points. 1 basis point is 1/100th of 1 percent. 100 basis points is equal to 1 full percent. An index fund with a fee of just 9 basis points, is a lot less expensive than a mutual fund with fees of 115 basis points. Don't ignore that! Over 40 years, that difference really adds up!**

be 0.0008. What that means is, if you have $1,000 invested in Vanguard Growth Index, which charges 8 basis points, your total fee for the year is 1,000 x 0.0008 or, (***drum roll please***), 80 cents! That's about as close to getting something for nothing as you're going to get. Yes, you can buy index funds and ETFs with extremely low expense ratios, like 0.08. I love buying low expense ratio investments because more of my money stays in my account. Not only does that money stay with me, but it also grows and multiplies over time. The money we pay out in fees is gone forever, never able to make us another penny.

Let me provide a simple example that will blow your mind: You want to buy a new car which has an invoice of $30,000. One dealer, Mr. A, will sell it for eight basis points over invoice. Another dealer, Mr. B, wants 160 basis points. Dealer A will charge $24 over invoice, while dealer B charges $480. (It's a no-brainer which dealer should get the sale.) Think of dealer A as an index fund, and dealer B as a mutual fund. Now, if you have a portfolio worth $30,000, and the index fund has a total expense of $24 per year, while the mutual fund has a yearly cost of $480, which fund will leave more money in your account? (This assumes both funds return the same, which they often do if they are very similar in makeup.) What if your portfolio was $300,000? In that case, the fees would be $240 or $4,800, respectively. Expenses make a big difference! Pay attention to what the costs are. Remember, fees must be paid every quarter. The less money paid out in fees, the more remains in the account to grow and multiply. *I want as close to 100% of my earnings to stay in my account.*

A managed account has broker fees added to the mutual fund fees. Be aware of all the fees associated with an account. *Remember, all the fees are paid out by YOU.*

Index funds are becoming very popular with investors because they are so inexpensive to own.

This math is a little tricky, so let's review. An expense ratio of 0.08, is 0.08 per 100, or 0.08 divided by 100, which is 0.0008.

To calculate your actual dollar cost for $1,000 invested at an expense ratio of 0.08, multiply 0.0008 by 1,000 to get 0.80, or 80 cents. For $10,000 that fee is 8 bucks! Even if you have $100,000, the fee will be just $80. By contrast, a mutual fund with a fee of 1.24%, will cost you $1,240 per year. If the mutual fund and the index fund both earn 9%, investors are way ahead of the game with the index fund. Remember, these fees are charged every year, so if an investor keeps the mutual fund for 10 years, it will cost him $12,400. (Probably more than that, as it will likely go up in value.) If the account eventually grows to a million dollars, the mutual fund fee will be $12,400 per year, while the index fund fee is only $800!

The reason this bit of math is so important is that over 40-50 years, the money not paid out in fees, stays invested, and compounds for your benefit. It could amount to a huge sum over time. Remember back in chapter one; I cited an example of a low expense ratio portfolio ending up with $700,000 more than its high expense ratio twin!

I find it stunning that people will study supermarket flyers to save a few pennies on a can of peas, but be totally oblivious to the fact that they may be cutting themselves out of tens of thousands, or even hundreds of thousands of dollars simply because of excessive fees built into their investment vehicles. *This little tidbit of information alone could save you enough to buy several new cars in retirement.*

I am not saying that mutual funds are not good. They are a fantastic concept, and people have, and continue to make billions of dollars with them. Some mutual funds have fabulous records, and brilliant managers. The truth is, index funds can be purchased and held for a lot less expense, so they should be considered. Active management does not guarantee better performance.

Here are a few examples of Index Funds (As of 8/31/16)
(Remember, these are not recommendations, just random selections for you to see.)
Huge amounts of reference materials are available for free on the Internet, at libraries, and via brokerage companies.

Index Fund	Ticker	1-year Return	5-Year Return	10-Year Return	Expense Ratio & Load
Fidelity Mid Cap Index Fund	FSTPX	13.84	14.67	n/a	.06 & 0
Vanguard 500 Index Fund	VFINX	11.82	14.49	8.82	.16 & 0
Schwab 1000 Index Fund	SNXFX	11.53	14.24	6.83	.29 & 0
Schwab International Index Fund	SWISX	1.08	6.44	0.9	.23 & 0

Personally, I like index funds. They allow me to participate in the market, while affording me good diversification at costs that are sometimes so low I find it hard to believe. Competition is driving down the costs even further, and we are the winners in this cost squeeze. I have found that my returns have improved simply by switching from buying individual stocks to index funds. It's been a lot less work and aggravation as well! My only complaint is that I failed to do it years ago.

Here are a few more examples of index funds: Try looking them up for research experience

VINIX	FUSEX	VFINX	NOSIX
DSPIX	SWPPX	PREIX	SIDIX
TRSPX	USSPX	SPFIX	GEQZX
NEIAX	PLSAX	PIIAX	SSPIX
FAEIX	PSIAX	SPIAX	PEOPX
SXPAX	WFILX	GRMAX	RYSOX

(These are not recommendations, just examples.)

ETF's

It's time to move on to explain ETFs, or exchange traded funds. ETFs are a type of mutual fund or index fund, except they can be traded all day, just like a stock. As an example, an investor may buy an oil ETF if she thinks that the price of oil will escalate during the day. An oil ETF will contain stocks of companies in businesses related to the oil industry. If, as the day wears on, the oil ETF goes up in price, she could sell it, and take her profit right then and there. Of course, every time an ETF is bought, and every time it is sold, a transaction cost is incurred. (By now you know how I feel about transaction costs.) If an investor is trading his portfolio on a regular basis, using ETFs can significantly increase his costs because every time he buys, he is charged a transaction fee.

Just like mutual funds, and index funds, ETFs come in every conceivable configuration. You can buy ETFs that reflect healthcare, energy, industrials, financials, consumer products, commodities, or almost any other class of equity. You can even buy an ETF that reflects the S&P 500.

Most of my investments are long-term, so I rarely trade them with any regularity. It doesn't bother me that I have to wait until the market has closed to sell a mutual fund or index fund. ETFs provide the option of buying and selling any time, just as if they were individual stocks. The ETF owner can monitor the price, and watch it rise and fall while the market is open. The ETF can be bought or sold any time while the stock exchange is open.

The one way all these vehicles are similar is that they allow an investor to dilute her risk in a basket of assets rather than having all her money in individual stocks or bonds. While many people prefer buying individual stocks or bonds, doing so usually requires a high level of skill, understanding, and experience. That old saying, 'don't put all your eggs in one basket', has been passed on from generation to generation for a good reason. It is a fundamental form of risk management. Risk is managed by not concentrating money in any one, or just a few, stocks or bonds. Fund investing is ideal for long-term retirement accounts.

Here are a few ETFs to look at (As of 8/31/16) (Remember, these are not recommendations, just random selections.)
Huge amounts of reference materials are available for free on the Internet, at libraries, and via brokerage companies.

ETF	Ticker	1-year return	5-year return	10 -year return	Expense ratio & Load
Vanguard Small Cap ETF	VBK	10.74	12.8	8.33	.08 & 0
Vanguard S&P 500 Growth ETF	VOOG	6.74	14.38	n/a	.15 & 0
Blackrock Core S&P Small Cap ETF	IJR	26.49	16.58	8.96	.12 & 0
Fidelity Nasdaq Composite Index	ONEQ	8.92	16.92	9.35	.21 & 0

Here are some more examples of ETF's:
These are not recommendations, just examples.
Use them to practice your research skills.

FDVV	FDRR	FDMO	FOAL
DOL	VXUS	URVTI	SCHX
SCHZ	SCHD	HDV	PFF
FVAL	PWV	MDYV	VOO
IVV	RSP	VLUE	DVY

Have some fun looking these ETF's up using your brokerage account, or one of the web sites I listed earlier. Notice that ETF's and Index funds have very low expense ratios.

What if there was a place an investor could go to analyze a mutual fund or ETF? What if that site could provide the following information?

- The expense ratio and the total expense cost per year for years 1-10
- A graph showing the growth of $10,000
- Morningstar rating. (This is a star rating with five stars being the highest.)
- Average annual return for one year, five years, and ten years.

- Average annual return since inception.
- Electronic prospectus. (A prospectus is a legal document required by the SEC, and it provides details about an investment offering. The final prospectus, which is also available on this site, provided details such as the offering price, number of shares issued, etc.)
- Annual report. (This is a legal document that explains the operations and financial condition of the investment.)
- Calculators to help you meet your investment goals.

What if all of this was available by a simple mouse click, and what if all this critical information was totally free?

Such a site does exist. It is completely free. An investor could work for years and never be able to accumulate and collate the data available here with just a computer and mouse.

What if this same site also provided information and teaching tools? What if it provided information about financial professionals, so investors can easily check on the person or firm they are thinking of using?

The information and educational materials on this site are simply breathtaking.

Why have you never heard about this site? Good question.

Look ... my objective is to help my family understand how to grow money. I don't sell anything or advise anyone.

I just try to facilitate investment education. I want my family and friends to have access to as much quality information and research as possible. Not everyone will tell you about these resources. The more investors use this free website and evaluate the various costs of ETFs and mutual funds, the more they will realize that they can invest their money with almost zero expense!

Ready? The site is: www.finra.org (Financial Industry Regulatory Authority)

There is a wealth of information like: fund analyzers, calculators, games, fraud avoidance, and much more.

Go there and spend some time exploring the site. Play with everything. Use the calculators. Analyze some mutual funds and ETFs. Get comfortable with the site and make it one of your favorite places. Educate yourself. Your homework assignment is to go to the website: www.finra.org. Click on _tools and calculators_, then click on fund analyzer. Once there,

WWW.FINRA.ORG

This is a wonderful website.

Lots of great information, calculators, and advice.

Do yourself a favor and bookmark it.

type in the name of a fund or ETF. Just for fun, type in VOO. That will bring up a Vanguard S&P 500 ETF. Look at the amount of information provided. Pay special attention to the expense information. For this particular fund, it is just five basis points. (100 basis points are one percent, so five basis points are just five one-hundredths of one percent!) That's only 50 cents per thousand! Everything else the fund gains is all yours!

Have some fun exploring this site. Just poking around this site will broaden your financial education immensely. Resources like this are truly an investors best friend.

Individual Stocks and Bonds:

Buying individual stocks can be extremely tempting. You might be at a cocktail party where someone talks about a stock they bought for 30 dollars which is now selling for $400. 'It was like hitting the lottery', they proudly exclaim. They explain how they *knew* the company was going to skyrocket. It's too bad you didn't get in. You should have bought it when they discussed it at the last cocktail party; blah blah blah. Let me assure you, I've been buying individual stocks for many years, and the odds of you hitting that kind of home run are extremely rare.

What we don't often hear at cocktail parties is the story about the stock that was purchased for 27 dollars and is now selling for 97 cents. That kind of debacle is not so much fun to chirp about. When a stock is purchased, the maximum loss potential is 100%. Believe it or not, certain options can lose more than 100%. Every individual stock has a different level of risk. Many stocks operate for years without a net profit. Some stocks carry huge debts on their balance sheets. Some stocks will quadruple in price while others will go to zero. Some stocks act just like bonds, paying regular and steady dividends year after year. The problem is that even the most seasoned investors cannot consistently pick winners and avoid losers. That's why most of my long-term retirement money is in index funds, mutual funds, and ETFs.

Selecting an individual stock or bond is much riskier than buying a mutual fund of stocks or bonds. I tried doing it for years. I was able to pick big winners, but not *all* winners. My losers pulled down my returns so that in the end, after long and tortuous hours of work, the S&P 500 index *beat me!* I'm not proud of that. It never made any sense to me that with all my hard work, discipline and in-depth understanding of the equity markets, I still couldn't beat a simple index fund! That has been my experience, and I am sharing that to save you time and to help you be a successful investor. (By the way, I'm not the only well-schooled investor who can't beat the S&P 500 index. Most mutual fund managers can't do it either!)

I know I'm not being overly optimistic about individual stock investing. I don't want to discourage anyone, but I have to be honest. Individual stocks are not easy. Even the very best investors cannot regularly beat the market. If that discourages you, maybe it should. *Remember ... when none other than Warren Buffett insists that 90% of the legacy he leaves to his heirs be invested in the S&P 500 index fund ... what does that tell us?* Just reread that sentence a few more times. Yeah, that's my advice. Reread that sentence until it truly sinks in.

When buying an individual stock, investors are buying a tiny piece of the entire company. When I say a tiny piece, I mean a very tiny piece. It is not uncommon for companies to have hundreds of millions of shares outstanding. A stockholder's tiny piece of that company may or may not pay a dividend.

The stock may or may not even make a profit. Many companies operate for years without showing a profit. When I buy an individual stock, I like to know as much about the company as I can. I want to know about the management team, the product or products the company produces, the sales, the profit margins, and the earnings per share. I also like to know the projected earnings per share for the next 5 to 10 years, if possible.

In addition to all of this, I like to know if the company is carrying a large amount of debt. When you buy shares in any company, you are buying the good, the bad, and the ugly. Believe me, I have bought some stocks that turned out to be very ugly. One stock I owned nearly went to zero when a foreign competitor stole their trade secrets. The competitor that stole those secrets was then able to manufacture and service the very things that they had contracted to buy from the company whose stock I owned. There is absolutely no possible way that I could have anticipated that debacle. The company was, and still is, a fine American corporation. There was never a reason to suspect that such espionage would crush them, and me in the process. I had a substantial amount of money in this one individual stock, and it collapsed to pennies. None of this was the fault of the company; all of it was the fault of a criminal act perpetrated by a foreign competitor. The fact that it wasn't my fault didn't matter one bit. I lost most of my investment. This loss was in my retirement account, and thus a blow to my plans.

When buying an individual stock, the risk of something unforeseen happening is always there. A great company may be doing a fabulous business, and then things change. If they fail to meet their earnings expectations for two or three quarters in a row, look out below! The price of that stock could collapse by 50% or more. Of course, the reverse is also true. A stock could have record earnings, tremendous growth, good public buzz, and the price could rise to shocking heights. The thing to understand is that individual stocks can be very volatile. They require skill to evaluate, confidence and nerve to hold onto, and constant vigilance to know if, and when the reason for owning them has changed. Just because Uncle Pete told you to buy XYZ in June, don't expect him to call, and tell you to sell in December when XYZ is in trouble, and is about to drop like a rock.

Similar things can happen when owning individual bonds. An individual bond is essentially a contractual loan to an entity at a specific interest rate. Loaning money to the United States Treasury carries very little risk. Investors are assured that the United States will pay. When loans are made in the form of a bond to a corporation, and the corporation does poorly or goes bankrupt, the investor may never get paid back. When corporations are on very thin ice financially, they typically pay a much higher percentage rate to entice lenders to loan them money. That higher rate of interest comes with a much higher risk. Many of these bonds are called "junk bonds." Who would buy a bond labeled junk? Millions do every day! They buy them because the bond has been able to return 7% interest in a 2% environment. An investor can get 2% with no risk in a U.S. Treasury bond, or shoot for more than three times that in a corporate junk bond, or junk bond fund. Many people will take the chance and hope for the best. Corporations need the money, and they are willing to pay a higher interest rate because they *must have the cash to do business*, and they hope the higher rate will entice lenders to make the loan.

Not all corporate bonds are junk. Many people have gotten, and stayed, rich by buying high-quality corporate bonds. Having said all that, I still prefer buying bond funds over individual bonds. I simply don't know enough to feel comfortable sinking a large amount of money in a single bond. You probably shouldn't either.

Just as mutual funds may contain dozens or even hundreds of individual stocks, bond funds could contain dozens or even hundreds of individual bonds. In either case, if a single stock or a single bond goes bankrupt, there will be only a limited impact on the fund itself. Owning a single bond that goes bankrupt, could wipe out the entire investment.

Here are a few Bond Funds to look at (as of 2/1/17)
(Remember, these are not recommendations, just random selections)
Huge amounts of reference materials are available for free on the Internet, at libraries, and via brokerage companies.

Bond Fund	Ticker	1-year return	5-year return	10 -year return	Expense ratio & Load
Pimco Long Duration Total Return	PLRIX	7.18	4.43	7.72	.5 & 0
Investco Multi Asset Income Fund Class A	PIAFX	12.36	6.21	n/a	.85 & 5.5
Doubleline Total Return Bond Fund	DBLTX	2.17	4.03	n/a	.47 & 0
Investco Corporate Bond Fund Class A	ACCBX	8.05	5.04	5.5381	.90 & 4.25

Bond funds come in many varieties. There are municipal bond funds, U.S. government bond funds, corporate bond funds, as well as international bond funds, junk bond fund, and many others. The choices are endless. I will list some more examples below. Practice looking them up and analyzing them.

Some more bond funds to research:

GNMFX	PTIAX	GMODX	NITEX
PONAX	GCMFX	HICOX	BBINX
SFBDX	PMZAX	DLINX	PONDX

(These are not recommendations, just examples.)

CHAPTER 6
Retirement Plans

N ow, let's look at 401(k) retirement plans and IRA retirement plans. These vehicles make it possible for almost anyone to accumulate huge sums of money on which to retire. The key is to start as early as possible and contribute regularly and significantly. Do not wait. Do not make excuses. Your retirement may indeed depend on one of these plans.

401(k)

An employer usually provides 401(k) plans. Sometimes the employer will match part of the employee's contribution into the 401(k). Always maximize your contribution into the 401(k) plan. This is especially true if by maximizing your contribution, that maximizes the employer's contribution as well.

Normally, I would advise that if something sounds too good to be true, it is. Such is not the case with 401(k) plans. Let me explain. What if someone said that there was a way to get a 10% - 20% return on

> **PROCASTINATION IS YOUR ENEMY**
>
> PROCRASTINATION IS YOUR ENEMY! NEVER PUT OFF SAVING FOR RETIREMENT. DO NOT WAIT A SINGLE DAY, WEEK, OR MONTH. DO IT NOW AND DO NOT STOP!

savings, just by stashing it aside? That most certainly sounds too good to be true; however, let me explain how the 401(k) works. Employees are allowed to invest up to $18,000 each year in a 401(k). (That goes up to $24,000 if you are age 50 or above.) In addition to that, the employer can also contribute to the employees 401(k) account. By the way, for people who are over 50, that extra $6,000 will help them catch up, especially if they got a late start building the portfolio.

Here is the part that almost seems too good to be true. The entire $18,000, (or $24,000 after age 50), that the employee contributes is completely tax-deferred. If you are in a 15% tax bracket, that is like getting a 15% return automatically. The government does not tax the money that goes into the 401(k). Wow! That means your retirement fund is being subsidized by other taxpayers. Of course, the term tax-deferred means just that. Eventually, when money gets withdrawn, taxes will be due. The great thing is, all that money continues to grow tax-deferred for the entire time it is in the 401(k). But, as they say in the infomercials, wait ... there's more! If the employer matches 3% of the employee's income, that's like getting an additional 3% return for free. So far, we're up to 18%, and we haven't even earned a penny from the market. If the investments earn 7%, that would be added to the 18%, providing a grand total of 25%. If anyone told me there was a way to do that, I would say it's simply too good to be true. **In the case of a 401(k), it is true, and it is an opportunity that you should not, and must not, miss out on. If you have the opportunity to invest in a 401(k) ... DO IT! Don't even think about it. Do not wait, do not procrastinate, and do not be afraid to lock this money away. You will never regret it!**

It is unlikely that employees will have a great deal of input as to the expenses incurred in the 401(k) plan, but that should in no way dissuade anyone from fully participating in the plan.

IRAs:

IRAs, also known as individual retirement accounts, are like 401(k) plans with some specific differences. For anyone aged 49 or younger, the maximum contribution to an IRA is $5,500 per year. For people 50 or older, that contribution goes up to $6,500 per year. You may contribute to an IRA even if you are participating in a 401(k) plan at work. I recommend doing both if you can. All the gains in the IRA are tax-deferred. Tax-deferred monies grow so much faster than taxable investments. That is why it is so important to begin a tax-deferred retirement savings plan as early as possible. Contributions to an IRA are tax-deferred if the income guidelines set forth by the IRS are met. These guidelines are easily available on the Internet. Investors should make sure they fall within the Federal guidelines. Checking with an accountant is a good idea. If an IRA is self-directed, like mine is, the investor will be able to control expense costs. If an IRA plan is not self-directed, or is managed by an insurance company, investment advisor, or broker, investors should let them know that expense ratios are a serious concern.

ROTH'S SOUND TOO GOOD TO BE TRUE!

Getting a chance to invest in an account from which TAXES will NEVER be due, sounds almost too good to be true. It is true though. A Roth IRA can provide you with tax free income.

Roth IRAs:

A Roth IRA is an investment vehicle that grows

tax-deferred for the entire time it is owned. The big difference between a Roth IRA and a traditional IRA is that the contributions put into the Roth are not tax deductible. The good part is that all the gains, forever and ever, are not taxed at all. This is another case of something sounding like it is too good to be true. **Imagine having a substantial Roth IRA, generating a wonderful income, and providing you that income with no taxes due! EVER! What a deal.**

There are income limits that restrict Roth IRA's. These limits vary from single filers to joint filers. Because these limits can change, it's best to check with an accountant to be sure you qualify. Currently, singles must have an adjusted gross under $133,000, and married filers under $196,000. If qualified, the limit is $5,500 per year, and that must be earned income, not passive income.

Although I have repeated this point many times throughout this book, it is important that I do it once more. **Time is the magic** that makes these things work with enormous power. If you plan to retire comfortably, then plan to be invested for *decades*. This is the reality that all investors must understand. Time and rate of return are the great multipliers of money. While you may not always be able to control your rate of return, you have *100% control over time*. Every year you postpone investing will diminish your fortune. I truly regret not starting my investments sooner.

The whole point of this book is to provide investment advice to my two adult sons, their wives, and so, by default, to my grandchildren. I love my family, and would never provide them with advice that I didn't believe with all my heart is good. Everything you read here is simply the advice that I have provided for my son James and my son Nicholas. I added an appendix at the end of this book, which will provide some information sources to enhance your knowledge.

Again, I am not, nor do I profess to be a financial advisor. The information I have presented here is simply a reflection of my experiences over the 40 years of investing that I have done. I provide this information because I wish that someone had enlightened me when I was in my teens or 20s. I was blissfully ignorant of this life-changing information, as millions of people are right now. There is no doubt that had this information been provided to me at a young age, I would be a multimillionaire today. I simply did not know any of this. I thought stocks were something that only wealthy people could be involved with. When I was in my teens and early 20s, the very last thing I thought about was that someday I would be in my 60s or 70s. I had no idea that money could grow and compound with such amazing results. I had no idea how valuable time was in the investment equation. I squandered time foolishly, letting years pass without my even knowing what I was missing out on. I wish somebody sat me down and explained all of this stuff to me a long time ago.

I know it now though, and I hope I have explained it adequately to you. It is very simple stuff. Don't complicate it. I advised my sons to get invested as soon as possible, invest in a broad market index like the S&P 500, and let that wonderful secret sauce called time do its magic. It is possible to invest in more than one index, and that is fine, as long as the investor knows what his/her objectives are, and what the objectives of those indexes are. There is an enormous amount of help available on the Internet. Much of that help is free. Some investors may feel they need professional advice, and that may be a good idea, especially in the beginning when setting a strategic trajectory is critical. Bear in mind that all investors should strive to keep expense ratios very low. The objective should be to keep as close to 100% of your investments as you can.

Investing today is totally different than it was 50 to 100 years ago. The amount of information that is at your fingertips through the Internet would have taken investors hours, weeks, and months to accumulate in days gone by. Everything about investing, from gathering information to executing trades has gotten easier and less expensive. Today, even the average investor can do it without the help of expensive advisors.

In the final chapters of this very short book, I would like to provide some food for thought, and a list of resources that will be very beneficial. Use these resources to further your understanding of this exciting and wealth-building process called investing.

CHAPTER 7

Amazing Numbers

Have you ever heard those stories of an old recluse that everyone assumed was just an unfortunate poor soul, living alone, obviously in poverty; and then it gets discovered that this person had millions of dollars? It seems like a totally impossible story to believe, but it happens frequently. The amazing thing is that the accumulation of millions of dollars is not all that difficult, even to reclusive old misers.

Let me cite some examples. Suppose someone could save the equivalent of **an inexpensive lunch a day for 45 years**. Let's say that inexpensive lunch costs $7.15 per day – that's a bit more than $200 per month. Let's say that was done for 45 years, earning 9% return on those savings, (no taxes or expenses included). **At the end of 45 years, that pile of assets would be worth $1,370,408.90**

Now the next scenario is rather unlikely, but if the portfolio earned 15%, the grand total would then be **$8,612,912.61. Yes, you're reading it right, 8.5 million dollars!!**

Bear in mind that if the $7.15 per day got stuffed into coffee cans, or under a mattress, the total would only be $117,438.75. Some people think keeping their money in cash is a safe bet. It's a pretty foolish bet. I'm going to provide a chart showing the difference in the amount of money an investor would accumulate at various rates of return. (These figures assume no taxes or fees.)

Returns from saving $7.15 per day: [a simple lunch) for 45 years]

(7%-11% are bolded because that is the average range of return from the S&P 500)

0% return:	**$117,438.75** (Saving the money and hiding it under the mattress.)
1% return:	**$147,402.03**
2% return:	**$187,662.72**
3% return:	**$241,976.59**
4% return:	**$315,857.67**
5% return:	**$416,779.08**
6% return:	**$555,209.51**
7% return:	***$745,737.12***
8% return:	***$1,008,686.90***
9% return:	***$1,372,365.09***
10% return:	***$1,876,169.09***
11% return:	***$2,574,889.85***
12% return:	**$3,544,654.41**
13% return:	**$4,891,119.88**
14% return:	**$6,760,752.39**
15% return:	**$9,356,324.85**

Take a very careful look at the numbers listed on page 109.

There will be a little over a hundred thousand dollars if the cash is squirreled away in a shoe box or under a mattress.

If invested at an average of 8%, that total rises to over a million!

The extra $900,000 comes from earnings on investments.

That is the power of compounding over time. Yes, it took 45 years, but that time was going to pass either way, why not let it make you a millionaire!!

Do you understand now why I am such a bug about not giving away 2% of my portfolio in fees? Just look at the difference 2% makes. For example: if you look at the preceding chart, at 7%, the return is $745,737.12, but **at 9% that return rises to $1,372,365.09!** *That is a difference of an astounding $626,662.80!! An extra 2% is a very big deal.*

Now: here is just one more piece of mathematics that needs to be understood. Brace yourself. I am about to blow *your mind! Remember I demonstrated how much an investor would have if she put the $7.15 per day in a shoebox or under the mattress.? I told you that it would add up to $117,438.75. That is the actual amount the saver tucked away in cash. Now, compare that with any of the invested return numbers. Let's use 9% as an example. The total in that pile is $1,372,365.09!! (No fees or taxes figured). When we subtract the $117,438.75; (the actual cash amount invested), from the $1,372,365.09 that was accumulated, we will find a difference of $1,254,926.34. Where did that 1.254 million dollars come from? You never pounded a nail for it. You never wrote a report for it, or treated a patient, or drove a truck, or fixed a computer, or waited on a customer. You never did a lick of work for it! It came from compounding. Only a little over a hundred thousand dollars was invested, but it wound up growing to over a million! Knowing this is like knowing one of the greatest secrets of the universe!*

Please, please, please ... re-read the previous paragraph. If after re-reading it you are still not convinced of the value of a tax deferred retirement account, and the power of compounding, then you might as well stop reading this now. I'll never convince you, and any further reading will be a waste of time.

Don't tell me or anyone else that you will never be able to retire because your job does not provide an employer paid pension. **Today, most people must set part of their income aside to make**

their own pensions. I'm sorry to have to report that, but it is the truth, and it's not as bad as you think. Many people have retired with nice pensions, only to live just a few years after they start to collect. If they die, in most cases, the pension fund is no longer obligated to pay out a penny. Guess what happens to the assets that were set aside to pay for that pension benefit. Unless the pensioner purchased an expensive option to insure the pension for a beneficiary, that money just stays in the pension plan. The pension plan hits the lottery when a pensioner dies prematurely, with no insurance option. The reason this happens is because a pension is essentially an annuity that is designed to pay out for a fixed number of years and then stop. Some people collect for just 2 years; some collect for 52 years. The pension fund has actuarial data to help it stay fully funded.

Now ... guess what happens to the $1,700,000 in your self-funded retirement account if you die early. It goes to your heirs! It is your legacy to do

ONE HUGE BENEFIT OF A SELF-FUNDED IRA ACCOUNT IS THAT IT DOES NOT DIE WHEN THE ACCOUNT OWNER DOES. MANY PENSIONS SIMPLY EVAPORATE UPON DEATH, BUT A SELF-FUNDED RETIREMENT ACCOUNT LIVES ON TO PROVIDE FOR YOUR HEIRS, OR WHATEVER IS DEAR TO YOU.

with as your hopes and dreams dictate. It goes to your spouse, children, church, or wherever you have arranged it to go. Those assets that have accumulated over time, stay after the investor dies. They don't just disappear. That is a HUGE benefit which is greatly underestimated in value. That is a very big thing, and another great reason to have a self-funded account.

Do you understand the difference? A pension is like an annuity. It simply pays a regular amount until death, at which point (in most cases), it stops paying. If the retiree wants to pass the pension on, that can often be done for a substantial insurance premium. That premium is deducted from the full pension benefit. A personal retirement plan is private money. If the account holder dies, the personal retirement plan lives on to nourish loved ones, or loved organizations. This is a very big deal, and far too little emphasis has been placed on that benefit.

Before I present a nice list of resources that will help enrich your investment education, I want to take you on a visit to the *factory*. There is a *factory* that has been producing investment myths for 100 years. These myths continue to live on even though there is little or no truth in them. That is why we must visit the bullshit factory. Rest assured that this trip is well worth the time and effort. Billions of dollars have been lost in the stock market simply because of these bullshit ideas

CHAPTER 8

The Bullshit Factory

Bullshit, Baloney, Half-Truths, and Other Nonsense Exposed

BS: Investing is very complicated and requires an enormous amount of skill and understanding. Just as the average person should not do brain surgery, no one should ever attempt to invest money without an advisor. Leave it to the professionals, only they have the expertise to be successful. The average person is just not smart enough to manage their own money.

Truth: *Investing is not brain surgery! In fact, being a successful investor can be one of the easiest things to do. Now that everyone has access to mutual funds, index funds, and ETFs, it's easy to set up a great portfolio that will allow investors to meet or beat some of the smartest people in the game! Even new investors can do better than many mutual funds. (And they can do all this with expense ratios that are lower than ever in the history of investing!)*

BS: Buying stocks is the same as gambling. The stock market is nothing more than a giant casino. It's possible to lose everything and wind up broke. Just buy Treasury bonds, or better yet, leave your savings in the bank where it will stay safe.

THE FACTORY

I AM SO HAPPY THAT YOU CAN VISIT THE FACTORY WITH ME.

THE FACTORY HAS BEEN PUMPING OUT BULL DROPPINGS FOR YEARS. SOME OF THAT BULL CONVINCES US TO DO THE EXACT OPPOSITE OF WHAT WE SHOULD DO. THAT IS WHY MUST TAKE THE TOUR. TRY NOT TO GET ANYTHING ON YOUR SHOES!

Truth: *The stock market has dramatically out-performed cash and bonds over the long term. The comparison is not even close. According to a graph published in the book: <u>Stocks for the Long Run</u>; by Jeremy J. Siegel;[9] a dollar invested in stocks in 1801 would be worth 12.7 million 200 years later, while bonds, gold, or treasury bills would be only worth a fraction of that.* **Conservative, careful, diversified funds** *will most likely continue to outperform bonds and cash, as they have done historically. Remember, inflation eats up part of our savings, so if we get 1% on our cash and inflation is 2%, we lose 1% by holding cash! It is a good idea to keep some cash and bonds in a portfolio. These assets tend to smooth out the volatility associated with stocks. Some cash allows the investor to take advantage of bargain prices when the market inevitably goes down.*

While it is true that some stocks are very risky and trading them is a lot like gambling, that is not how I invest, and I would never encourage anyone to invest in risky stocks either. I consider retirement money in the bank, a lot riskier than retirement money in a conservative index fund of stocks. The

---

9 Siegel, Jeremy, J (2008) *Stocks for The Long Run* New York, NY McGraw Hill Figure 1-1 p.8

reason is, the likelihood of an average investor having enough money to retire on from bank interest is not good, while one invested in an index fund such as the S&P 500, will most likely do great.

GREED

Greed is one of the most dangerous emotions relative to investing; as it increases stupidity proportionally, as it decreases logic, and mathematical reasoning.

BS: The best thing to do is time the market. It is easy and smart to buy low and sell high. By timing the market, anyone can outperform all the indexes. Always buy at the bottom and sell at the top.

Truth: *No one is smart enough to time the market, and no one ever has been. Some people have been lucky, and so it looks like they have timed the market, but they were just lucky. No one knows when the market will have a big run up or a steep drop down. What we do know is that over a very long period of time, the S&P 500 has returned about 10% per year. Over 40 or 50 years, the market will gyrate up, down, and sideways. While this can be exasperating, it tends to be more profitable to just stay in, rather than trying to get in and out at the right times.*

BS: Technical indicators will always tell an investor when to buy and when to sell. Just watch the charts, know the patterns, and it's easy to know exactly what the market will do. That is how the real professionals make money in the stock market.

Truth: Technical indicators can be helpful, but they cannot predict the movement of the market with absolute precision. Most technical patterns are backward looking and tell you what has happened in the past. Some people feel they can predict a future action based on the past movements. Don't bet your retirement on it.

BS: Don't worry about paying an upfront load on a mutual fund. Investors in load funds pay more because the fund is better than no-load funds, and will have a much higher return. If it cost more, it must be better.

Truth: Actually, load funds often do no better than no-load funds. Why pay up to 6% loads on an investment? That means only part of your money gets invested! AVOID THEM!

BS: Penny stocks can make a fortune quickly.

Truth: *Many stocks become penny stocks as they head to bankruptcy. Some penny stocks do not make money and never will. Some penny stocks, which seem like amazing bargains at 13 cents, will sink to just 6 cents. That's a 50% loss no matter how you cut it. Most penny stocks are not investments; they are speculations.*

BS: The best time to buy a stock is when someone provides a good tip.

Truth: *Most hot stock tips don't pan out. Don't buy a stock until you have done your due diligence. (Due diligence takes a huge amount of time, effort, and know-how.)*

BS: There are systems and newsletters out there that can provide secrets on how to get market returns of 40% or more. While it does cost money to get these systems and newsletters, they are worth it because they work.

Truth: *If it sounds too good to be true, it is too good to be true. I know of no system or newsletter that* *can safely guide you to 40% returns. If there was a way to do that, why doesn't everybody do it? Look, the truth is, investors are vulnerable to fantastic claims, and sellers of those claims know it. I make my money the old-fashioned way, by trying to replicate the overall market returns year after year. It is slow, steady and boring. Chasing after unrealistic gains have caused more heart-ache than almost any other investing mistake. Greed often seduces investors to do things that are foolish and illogical. After investors have lost their money, they cannot imagine how they ever got sucked into the scheme.* **Greed is one of the most dangerous emotions relative to investing, as it increases stupidity proportionally, as it decreases logic, and mathematical reasoning.**

BS: Options[10] are where the real money is made.

Truth: *Options are a very tricky business. Investors need to know all about volatility, time decay, premiums, and underlying values. In addition*

---

10 Options are a way to bet which way the price of an equity, like a stock, will move. Options can give you a right to buy or sell a stock at a pre-determined price. These are complicated derivatives, and not recommended for the novice, or un-skilled investor.

to that, the investor must know how to evaluate the data known as: delta, gamma, theta, vega, and rho. If this is all Greek to you, you are not ready for options. P.S. Some options can lose more than 100% of a stock's price.

BS: Stocks only go up when the economy is good, and the market is bullish.

Truth: *Stocks go up and down for a variety of reasons. One reason a stock goes up is earnings. When a company has good earnings, and those earnings are growing every quarter, year after year, investors will bid up the shares of that stock. These stocks may continue to rise even when the market is flat or down. What investors want, is to share in the future earnings growth for years to come. It is true that stocks tend to go up when the economy is strong, and the market is bullish. Even stocks that are less than perfect can rise in these conditions. The reverse is also true, that is, in bear markets, good stocks get punished right along with the bad ones. It would be great if we were only invested in bull markets and in cash for bear markets. Since that is virtually impossible, I tend to stay invested and ride out the ups and downs.*

BS: Don't worry about what a broker or financial advisor charges to manage an equity account. They know what they are doing and will easily make that fee up by getting higher returns than an average investor could possibly get without them.

Truth: *Maybe ... maybe not. Many managed accounts do not even do as well as the S&P 500 index, and anyone can buy that index with a mouse click. Some managed accounts do better, but very few consistently beat the market. One thing is certain: The fees paid are gone for good. Everyone in this business plays for keeps. I prefer to keep as much of my investments as I can. I don't like sharing my hard-earned money on fees. That doesn't make me greedy, just frugal. Over very long time periods, lower fees and low expenses can make a huge difference in how much you retire with. Failure to focus on how much it costs to be invested is like trying to win a foot-race with a backpack full of rocks*

BS: The only true investments of real value are gold, silver, and real estate.

Truth: *Gold, silver, and real estate can all be hedges against inflation. They can even experience periods of terrific returns, but they can also experience long periods of time where they remain stagnant or even shrink in value. Ask anyone who bought real* *estate in the bubble of 2007-2008. It didn't just go down, it crashed, putting many careless investors into bankruptcy. If someone bought gold in 2011 for $1,921, they would still be waiting for any return today. When dealing with commodities like gold and silver, it is critically important that those commodities are purchased at the right time and the right price. You are dependent on the price going higher than the price they were purchased for. Investors who buy when the price is high, may go for years without a profit, as these commodities pay no dividends. There are many funds that focus on real estate or precious metals. If Investors feel they need exposure to gold, silver, or real estate, mutual funds are available that can at least help diversify the risk of investing in them. Of the three, I prefer real estate, though I am not opposed to holding small amounts of gold as a hedge.*

BS: Technology and health care are where the big money is made.

Truth: *The reality is that various sectors do well at different times. There will be times when technology is hot, and it is almost impossible not to make money while being invested in that sector. There are times when healthcare is hot, and that sector will do well during those periods. The whole idea of diversification is that a portfolio is invested in multiple sectors so that as one is experiencing a bull market and another a bear market, the portfolio returns will be smoothed out by owning some of each sector. One of the reasons I like to invest in the S&P 500 Index is that it contains some of every sector of the economy.*

BS: Find mutual funds that made over 20%, and jump right in. That's the kind of fund that will make a ton of money. They will be listed in many of the financial magazines.

Truth: *Some mutual funds will beat the market by a lot one year then fail to repeat that performance the next year. I am not smart enough to know who will win and when they will win. (Most people probably aren't either.) I do know that betting on last year's winners is not always a great idea. Some mutual funds just get lucky, and that luck resulted in a one-time stellar performance. It may not get repeated again for years. I also know that many mutual funds simply do not even return as much as an index fund of the S&P 500.*

BS: The only safe place for hard-earned money is in the bank.

Truth: *The dirty little secret is inflation. If inflation is 2%, investments must make at least that to stay even. This is very important to understand because the future value is discounted by inflation. Future value is further discounted by expenses. This is where the "I want to keep my money safe" crowd makes huge mistakes. They stick their money in the bank and feel quite content as it deteriorates in buying power! "At least I know my money is safe," is their mantra, all the while it is like storing cheese and having the mice nibble away at it unseen! That money may be reduced in value after inflation and taxes. To grow in value, investments must be greater than the inflation rate. History has shown us that, over long periods, (10-40 years), stocks far outperform money in the bank. It isn't even close.*

BS: I really haven't lost anything if I don't sell my position.

Truth: *The investing game is always played "for keeps." If someone buys $10,000 worth of a stock and it goes to zero, they will lose that money for good. There are no "do-overs." There is no one to run to and seek "fairness." If a stock has lost 20%, don't just assume it will return to where it was purchased. It might, then again, it might drop another 20%. An investor needs to know if all* *the reasons he bought the stock are still valid. If all the reasons he bought the stock are no longer valid, then it makes sense to sell it and move on. An individual stock is not like a broad-based index fund that follows the market up and down. Stocks can go bankrupt but mutual funds rarely do.*

BS: I can make a ton of money "day trading". I just buy low, sell high, and repeat. Easy Peasy!

Truth: *Very few people make money day trading. Markets are fickle and random. When flipping a coin 500 times, about 250 will be heads, and 250 tails. Occasionally the numbers may change a little, but when repeated over and over, the odds remain constant. When we buy a stock, it might go up or it might go down. Sometimes we win, sometimes we lose. Every time we trade, we pay 2 fees. One to get in, and one to get out. To be successful, our winning trades need to outweigh our losing trades after all fees are paid. Don't quit your day job, you're probably going to need it!*

BS: Only financial professionals have the expertise to manage investments. This is no game for amateurs.

Truth: *Since even the best professionals cannot consistently beat the S&P 500 benchmark, and since **any amateur** can buy that benchmark, and buy it at an extremely low cost, it seems that the amateur can do quite well on their own. If an investor prefers to own mutual funds that are professionally managed, there are many low cost, managed, mutual funds that can be purchased directly. Millions of investors do it on their own with great success.*

The problem with myths and half-truths is exactly that; they are often half true. These myths can persist for decades and cause people to make very costly mistakes. They tend to be construed by personal prejudices and experiences that people have had over the years. Just as most prejudices lead to illogical and ridiculous conclusions, these financial myths do exactly the same thing. We could spend all day here at the factory, for it produces a prodigious amount of bull droppings. It is important to understand, that just because something has been said over and over for years, that does not necessarily make it true. I like to run these myths through the fine sieve of logic and mathematics. Once logic and mathematics are applied to these concepts, many of them simply melt away. Investing is best done with a sober, objective, and unemotional mind. If you feel excitement one way or the other when investing, take a deep breath, have a cup of tea, and do nothing.

CHAPTER 9
Final Words

I have kept this text short and to the point, for good reasons. The primary reason is, I wanted it to be an easy read. Anyone can breeze through my book in a short time. This book contains information that, unfortunately, is not known or understood by most people in this country. I am astounded at how little the average person knows about something as potentially life changing as investment finance.

Not knowing what is in this book could cost you the opportunity of a lifetime. That opportunity is the ability to grow investments large enough, so they will provide a comfortable retirement income. I certainly wish that I knew this information 50 years ago. I did learn it eventually, and I'm thankful for that, however by coming late to the party, I was not able to take full advantage of that magical, secret sauce called time. Time is the leverage that moves financial mountains. ***Do not waste another second.*** I had to learn the hard way, but you have the advantage of looking behind the curtain to see how things work. Take advantage of this knowledge, and make yourself a pile of assetts that will produce a wonderful retirement income.

Growing money tax-deferred is not a good deal...it is a GREAT DEAL!! Do it! Do it now and keep doing it until it hurts. Don't look back; just keep adding to the pile. Increase it every time you can. No one can time the market. It's almost impossible to buy at the bottom or sell at the top. Money is made by being in and staying in. Simple, boring, counterintuitive but true.

There is a feeling that once you experience, will change you forever. *That feeling comes the first time you realize that a pile of assets can earn as much as you make in a weekly paycheck. The sudden realization that a pile of investments can make you as much as you made for a week of swinging a hammer, working at the office, selling cars, seeing patients, or fixing computers; is life changing. As your investment pile grows, it generates as much money as a month's work. Eventually, and this is the "ah ha" moment, you realize that your investments are earning as much as an entire year of work! At this point, you understand what it means to be financially independent. The financial mass you have accumulated will generate enough money to live comfortably without ever having to work another day! I cannot over-emphasize how powerful these realizations are!*

*Most people must work to make enough money to live. The concept of earning money every week, month, or year, simply by having an investment portfolio, is not one that everyone intuitively understands. Since most people do not start out with a large chunk of wealth that generates income, they don't have that reference point. When people are living paycheck to paycheck, it's hard to imagine that substantial amounts of money can be earned by not working. Most working people don't understand how easy it is to accumulate a million dollars or more. Investing tax deferred over decades will provide that large chunk of wealth. **When that realization hits someone for the first time ... they will never be the same.** They will finally **"get it."** People who "get it", will understand everything I have been trying to tell you with this book. It takes **time** to accumulate enough to begin seeing results. That is why so many people simply do not stick with it. Please trust me on this point. Invest 10% to 15% of your earnings per year. Things will go slow at first, but eventually, that pile of money will be impresive. One day, the balance will exceed $100,000, and then the fun starts. You will be on the way to building a million dollar pension fund.*

Before we part company, you should know a tiny bit about this great and mysterious thing called the stock market, and the people who make their fortunes from it.

I remember when I was a child, long before the digital age, and long before the days of being able to record broadcasted programs, a person got to see a special movie on television just once or twice a year. There were very few networks, so they could decide when to show those special movies. One such movie was called the Wizard of Oz.[11] Everyone would gather around the black and white TV with great awe and anticipation as Dorothy, the Tinman, the Lion, the Scarecrow, and Toto the dog made their perilous way to see the great and wonderful wizard. After exciting adventures, they eventually found the wonderful wizard. The great and wonderful Oz was a frightening and powerful apparition. The apparition was full of sound, fury, and power. The great and powerful Oz had all the answers to all the questions that anyone could possibly ask. Just when everyone was completely mesmerized by the infallibility of the great Wizard,

Once you realize that you can make a week's, pay, a month's pay, or even a year's pay just by having money invested … your life will never be the same. You will finally "get it". You will finally understand that you can earn money passively, and eventually rely on it for retirement.

---

11 The Wizard of Oz is a 1939 Musical produced by Metro-Goldwyn- Mayer. It was based on the novel: The Wonderful Wizard of Oz, by Frank Baum.

Toto, the dog, pulled back a curtain and exposed a meek and mild man working the controls that animated the illusion. The great and powerful Oz was nothing but a giant illusion. If everyone believed the illusion, the great Oz had tremendous power. Once he was exposed, and it was evident that he was an ordinary man, his power evaporated.

Such is largely the case with many financial experts. We give them great power because we believe that, somehow, they know what the markets will do, and we think that they can protect our investments from harm. We want to believe that they have such great powers. We want to believe that they have near magical insights that can protect our investments from all harm and diminishment. I remember when I hired a large firm to manage my humble portfolio. I remember thinking that there was absolutely nothing to worry about because I had professionals watching out for me. When the great recession of 2008 occurred, I watched in horror as my retirement savings was cut in half! Where were these guys?? Hey ... I'm getting killed here! That's what I thought. I was certain, those guys in fancy suits knew so much about the stock market and investing, they would get my money out safely before any market meltdown. I might lose a few bucks, but they would get me out long before any giant losses. After all, they did great when the market was going up. I just assumed they had all the answers, all the tools, and all the insights to protect me. *They didn't.*

Now, I don't blame them. (Although I did at the time.) I was invested aggressively to make the most amount of gain I could in the market. They did as I instructed them to do. I just thought that somehow, they had powerful information that would save me. I was paying them well, so I assumed that they would never allow anything bad to happen to my money. Somehow, even if the mean old stock market wanted to hurt me, my professional money managers would gird their loins, draw out their swords, and protect me and my money with all their might. **They did not.** I lost 50% of my money.[12] Those wonderful wizards of finance didn't know what was about to happen any more than I did! *They still charged me almost 2% in fees for managing my gut wrenching losses!*

Allow me to pull back the curtain on the financial management sector. They have no idea if, or when, the market may crash, or when it might explode to the upside. When it rises, they will accept our praises and when it collapses they will reassure us that things will be okay. They will assure us that all will be well, and tell us not to panic or sell. Their power is largely illusionary. You believe in them of course, so you do as they say, and sometimes you should; as they have seen all this before, and so, by

---

12 I fired my advisors and took over the management of my own account. I regained all of my losses, and went on to double the portfolio value from there.

knowing the past, they tend to guess at the future. I am not saying that they do not have experience and some understanding, they do. They just do not possess superhuman insights. They cannot predict the future, and so they cannot guarantee anything. They are somewhat like the Wizard of Oz, a great and wonderful illusion. In fairness to them, they never actually tell us that they fully understand the markets, nor do they guarantee that our investments won't go down. When you visit them though, and they sit regally behind big mahogany desks, wearing expensive clothes, and surrounded by computer displays, we jump to our own conclusions: They *must* know a lot more than we do. We should pay them to manage our money. Just look at how rich *they* appear. This is what success looks like! One thing about them is real ... the fees you pay them. That I can assure you is no illusion. Investors can pay those fees for 40 or 50 years, but they don't have to. I have tried to show you ways of managing investments for little or nothing. Always remember that the objective is to reach critical mass. Critical mass is the amount of money required to live life without work. The process is not a great and incomprehensible mystery. Anyone can do it. Reaching critical mass happens much faster when expenses are kept as low as possible.

One more quick point before we part company. Every investor should plant two little rows of lettuce seeds. I am serious. You really should do this experiment. It is easy to do, and you won't get the full benefit if you just read this and don't actually do it.

The seeds can be planted in a flower pot in your house or apartment. Plant the seeds in two separate rows. In row one, just plant, water, and watch. (Be sure they get a bit of sunlight.) In row two, plant, water, and once the green shoots come up, dig them out and move them to different positions in the row. Do this several times during the growing cycle. Eventually, there should be enough lettuce for a tiny salad, but before you harvest that little garden, please note which row did better. All the extra fussing you did in row two did nothing to improve the results. All the digging and replanting was an exercise in futility. Lots of effort for no gain.

Such it is with investments. Trying to buy and sell with hopes of timing the market will often leave an account with less than if it would have had by doing nothing. The lettuce needs time to grow. It doesn't need constant fussing. Investments need time; they don't require constant hyperactive attention. I am not saying they do not require attention; they simply do not need overactive intervention. This is a very important concept to understand. A great deal of money is lost just because people can't resist fussing around with their investments. Patience, Patience, Patience. This is a game of patience. A farmer doesn't visit his cornfield and fuss around with the baby corn stalks. He, (she), plants, waits, and hopes for good weather. Some years he does well, and some years he does poorly. He knows that some things are out of his control. Just as the farmer cannot control the weather, you cannot control the market. Your responsibility is to get the seeds(capital) in the ground, so that growth can begin. You will have good years and bad years, but if capital is left in a box, or the farmer leaves his corn in a barrel, there is no hope of gain. The farmer does not want to end the season with a barrel of unplanted corn seeds; he wants truckloads of corn! Good investment returns, and good harvests require planning, planting, and waiting. *We do not plant today and eat tomorrow.* Everything takes time to grow. Nature teaches us that we can multiply our assets with time. Growing a portfolio to critical mass is like growing an entire orchard. Building a substantial orchard could take decades. As the years pass, the orchard grows, with profits, (dividends), used to buy more land, trees, and equipment. Eventually, the orchard is big enough to provide a lifetime of income. Portfolios grow in the same way.

(All this is done automatically with index funds.) It will take a lot of time. I know I have made this point over and over, but I do so because it is true and essential to understand. Get started. Keep adding to the portfolio. Save as much as you can. Be patient, the result is worth the wait!

A few words about why we have capital markets. Businesses and industries become established, grow, and expand on the mother's milk of capital. Capital is money. Building a factory could cost millions, with much more needed for employees, machinery, tools, and supplies. Very few people or organizations have the enormous resources to create such an enterprise without public participation. A company can sell tiny pieces of itself to raise the capital required. That allows us to own a tiny piece and share in the fortunes and misfortunes of the enterprise. That is the essence of capitalism. Capitalism allows these businesses to come into existence through the magic, the wonder, and the power of capitalization.

Countries with strong capital markets can grow and prosper rapidly. In areas of weak or nonexistent capital markets, economic activity suffers. When we invest, we become a little part of the capitalist system that helps create wealth and prosperity. Hopefully, it will greatly improve your personal wealth and prosperity. We are never just investing in a few letters on the stock exchange and hoping that the price goes up for some magical reason, and we benefit. No, we are investing in companies, people, managers, and CEOs. We are investing in enterprises that create jobs and wealth. We are investing in the engines that drive the economy forward.

As these companies grow and prosper, they need people to plan, build, develop, sell and transport their products. Millions of jobs are created, and in many cases, dividends are paid out to those who chose to invest. Of course, it's not a perfect system, but it is a system that has helped the United States of America become the richest and most powerful nation the world has ever seen. I sure hope that my helping you to understand this topic a bit better will result in your increased wealth and well-being.

Following this final chapter is an appendix where I provide some resources to consider for "extra credit." There are hundreds, and probably thousands of books written about investing. I have an extensive financial library that I maintain. I apologize in advance to all the authors of wonderful books that I do not list here. I simply want to provide a short list of excellent resources that will be very helpful for anyone desiring to further their education and understanding of modern investments. This small selection will provide a valuable education. I would encourage you to read these books to develop a better understanding of investing. Educate yourself. This stuff is not difficult to learn and understand.

I truly hope that I have helped to get you excited about building your personal fortune, and broadening your understanding of all things financial. I sincerely wish you the very best.

Be sure to bookmark the 2 websites I list below:

> **www.investor.gov** *(SEC's office of investor education and advocacy. Education and fraud protection.)*
> **www.finra.org** *(Financial Industry Financial Authority)*

These sites are maintained by government and non-government employees to provide a wealth of information, analysis, and calculation.

These sites should be an integral part of your investing education. They are free and easy to navigate. The tools are indispensable. The educational sections are easy to understand and are presented at a level that does not require a math or business background.

APPENDIX

AAII Journal: American Association of Individual Investors. 625 North Michigan Ave., Suite 1900, Chicago, IL 60611

Bogle, John C. (2007). <u>The Little Book of Common Sense Investing: The Only Way to Guarantee Your Fair Share of Stock Market Returns)</u>. John Wiley & Sons, Hoboken, New Jersey

Fisher, Ken, & Hoffmans, Lara. (2011). <u>Debunkery</u>. John Wiley & Sons, Hoboken, New Jersey

Greenblatt, Joel. (2010). <u>The Little Book That Still Beats The Market</u> John Wiley & Sons, Hoboken, NJ

Kelly, Jason. (2004). <u>The Neatest Guide to Stock Market Investing</u>. Penguin Group, New York, NY

Lynch, Peter. (1989). <u>One Up on Wall Street</u>. Simon & Schuster, New York, NY

Marks, Howard. (2013). <u>The Most Important Thing Illuminated</u>. Columbia University Press. New York, NY

Mladjenovic, Paul. (2009). Stock Investing for Dummies. Wiley Publishing, Inc. Hoboken, NJ

Morningstar. How to Select Winning Stocks. Wiley & Sons, Inc. Hoboken, NJ

O'Shaughnessy, James, P. (2012). What Works on Wall Street. McGraw Hill, New York, NY

Peris, Daniel. (2013). The Dividend Imperative. McGraw Hill, New York, NY

Pysh, Preston. (2012). Warren Buffett's Three Favorite Books. Pylon Publishing

Robins, Tony. (2014). MONEY Master The Game Simon &Schuster, NY, NY

Solin, Daniel R. (2011). The Smartest Portfolio You'll Ever Own. Penguin Group, New York, NY

Tyson, Eric. (2004). Mutual Funds for Dummies. Wiley Publishing, Hoboken, NJ

INDEX

tips 120
two percentage points
14
Tyco 54
Vanguard Growth Index
81

Warren Buffett 26
withdrawal rate 13
Wizard of Oz 132,135
Yahoo Finance 75

Made in the USA
Lexington, KY
14 April 2018